ESCAPE FROM
BERLIN

The

Report

Love great sportswriting? So do we.

Every month, Pitch Publishing brings
together the best of our world through
our monthly newsletter — a space for
readers, writers and fans to connect over
the books, people and moments that make
sport so captivating.

You'll find previews of new releases,
extracts from our latest titles, behind-the-
scenes interviews with authors and the
occasional giveaway or competition thrown in
for good measure.

We also dip into our back catalogue to
unearth forgotten gems and celebrate timeless
tales that shaped sporting culture.

Scan the **QR code** and join the growing Pitch
Publishing reader community today.

ESCAPE FROM
BERLIN

ENGLAND'S
BERT
SPROSTON
AND THE
FOOTBALL REFUGEE

JOHN LEONARD

First published by Pitch Publishing, 2026

1

Pitch Publishing
9 Donnington Park, 85 Birdham Road
Chichester, West Sussex, PO20 7AJ
www.pitchpublishing.co.uk
info@pitchpublishing.co.uk

Set in Adobe Caslon 11.9/18.2pt

Typeset by Pitch Publishing

Cover design by Olner Design

Printed and bound in India by Replika Press Pvt. Ltd.

The authorised representative in the EEA is
Easy Access System Europe OÜ, Mustamäe tee 50, 10621 Tallinn,
Estonia gpsr.requests@easproject.com

A CIP catalogue record for this book is available from the British Library

ISBN 978 1 83680 279 2

Papers used by Pitch Publishing are from
well-managed forests and other responsible sources

CONTENTS

INTRODUCTION:
PARALLEL LIVES ENTWINED

A MAGNIFICENT beast hisses at Berlin Zoologischer Garten station. No roar of a lion, the cackle of a hyena, the cries of chimpanzees or the chest-thumping of a gorilla. On a German autumnal morning, an iron horse fires up its engines. Nazi storm troopers, SS and Gestapo prowl alongside on the platform. None realise they are guarding a football special.

An anxious teenager climbs aboard. His name is Rolf Friedland. The passenger train is bound for the Channel coast. Rolf makes one more check of his paperwork and all is in order. His carriage shakes violently as the steam engine roars to life. Rolf is Jewish. The men in Nazi uniform step back from the platform edge. This time, they leave him alone. He is free to go.

A station porter's whistle blows, the train's engine driver sounds its whistle. Slowly but surely the wheels grind on the tracks as it trundles out of the station in an enveloping cloud of steam. Quite whether the young passenger will be enveloped into the welcome arms of the English people a few hours later is open to question.

Rolf is going to a football match in London. Just an awayday with legions of fans? Not at all. He has no intention of returning to Germany. He aims to claim asylum. It is October 1938. Nazi persecution of German Jews is intensifying and his train journey is the beginning of an unlikely ride to freedom.

The adventure's seed was planted months earlier as he took his place in Berlin's Olympiastadion. All, almost all, cheered to the heavens as an English football team made the Nazi salute. Hours later, one of those proud Englishmen agreed to help the teenage football fan escape the Nazis. Bert Sproston secured his visa for the UK, saving his life. In an era of intolerance, one man's tolerance shone through.

Quite how an England footballer saved a stranger's life is one of the more curious but uplifting episodes in the tale of a shameful day in English sporting history. Proud Englishmen giving the Nazi salute in an Olympic stadium before a game of international football? Well, just how do you address Adolf Hitler? 'Don't bother, don't worry,' might be the glib answer for the 21st century. At the very least, just deploy the good old-fashioned British stiff upper lip. But, back in the 1930s, this quandary posed something of a diplomatic and political headache for the British government and UK sports bodies, not least the Football Association.

To the anxious teenager boarding his train from Berlin some five months later the infamous football match gave him an unlikely opportunity to escape tyranny. Rolf Friedland succeeded. For Bert Sproston, his chance meeting with the teenager brought pride and redemption. No need to dwell on the order to give a Nazi salute before a game of football. Certainly, no need to dwell on a gesture given in honour of a man he allegedly dismissed as an 'evil little twat'.

As his train rattled along the congested tracks out of Berlin, Rolf sat back in his seat briefly reflecting on living through a traumatic few years in his home city. An uncertain future lay ahead. He hoped his bold bid for freedom might avoid hitting the proverbial buffers. It did so thanks to a professional footballer – their separate lives becoming entwined.

His mind drifted back to the cold, dark night of January 1933 when the Nazis took power – the time an intense chill swept through Berlin. Nothing to do with the winter weather. Not even a roaring log fire would bring genuine warmth as a boisterous child shivered. His parents shivered too, but not from the cold. Events relayed by the fireside radio gave them the chills. Germany had changed forever and changed for the worse. Soon tens of millions would be dead, hundreds of millions worldwide.

Rolf pulled over the warming blankets, drifting into sleep and dreamt of sport. But no night of glory under the lights for the country of his birth. Instead, he yearned for an escape from Germany. Every one of Rolf's waking hours threatened to drift into a nightmare. Jubilant Nazis declared 30 January 1933 as *Tag der Machtergreifung*, the day of seizing power. Germany's ailing president, Paul von Hindenburg, invited Adolf Hitler to form a cabinet. Once he did so, no one was safe, certainly not the Jewish community. Adalbert and Charlotte Friedland began to make plans for their young family; escape plans from a country they once called home.

Nobody summed up Rolf's predicament better than his future wife, Eva. The pair never met in their native Berlin. They fell in love as refugees making a new life in post-war London. Eva reflected with a strong degree of understatement, 'To be a Jewish teenager in 1933 was no fun. The arrival of the deadly Nazi regime threw its big shadows over our lives.'

In a weird sense, nothing had really changed in Germany. Nazis had been on the ascendancy for years and Jews were the victims of their hateful ideology. Throughout the 1920s, the Nazi narrative proved more and more popular. Extremist parties, whether the Nazis on the right or communists on the left of politics, attracted German voters in their millions. They exercised their democratic rights but democracy was under threat. Germans suffered humiliation in defeat in the Great War. Germany had little experience of democracy. Voters perversely flocked to parties declaring that it had failed. The Weimar Republic of Germany tottered on the brink of collapse. 'Germany first!' was a Nazi slogan. Anti-Semitism and conspiracy theories citing the power of 'world Jewry' became rife.

Just as if he needed a reminder, Rolf was soon expelled from school. His expulsion had nothing to do with any accusations of poor behaviour, failing to deliver his homework on time or fights in the playground. He was a model pupil. No, the very fact he was Jewish was enough to bar him from the school gates. From then on, the resourceful teenager needed to be self-educated. His family helped, then they disappeared and made their successful bid for freedom.

Hundreds of miles away an English teenager rose for the day ahead as sleet and snow danced outside on the same grim winter's day. There was no political chill, just the predictable wintry weather. Bert Sproston was beginning life as an apprentice plumber in Sandbach, Cheshire. He wanted to become a professional footballer, just like his eldest brother, Jack. Even playing football on dodgy pitches for a living was preferable to fixing frozen pipes.

Bert believed that he could do better than Jack, once a promising player with Port Vale. 'What? Port Vale! Who are they? Where are they?' Bert jokingly asked Jack. The Potteries club was based just 20 miles down the road from Sandbach in Hanley, Stoke-on-Trent.

It had struggled to break through the frozen wastes of the lower reaches of the Football League. Bert eyed life in English league football's top tier. International recognition? Good for young Bert to be ambitious.

A few clubs had their eye on him. For now, he made do with playing for beer money in the Cheshire County League. Not that he drank alcohol, he was too young. The ambitious footballer made do with life collecting his tools and rods, trudging to work as a plumber, also aching with tiredness and pain on his way to matches and training sessions. For a time, joining his brothers in the building trade seemed a more realistic career option than playing professional football.

As winter weather gripped rural Cheshire, recession still bedevilled Britain and afflicted the global economy. Germany, a nation resentfully paying off reparations from the Great War, struggled more than other Western countries. The German people, by no means most of them, swallowed the populist pill. The fascists, the Nazi Party, told everyone that they would solve their country's economic ills, that they would restore pride and put a lot more reichsmarks in the German people's pockets.

How? Plenty of people to blame for their woes, lots of scapegoats. These included their political rivals, the communists along with intellectuals in their university citadels, the established elite of the day. Above all for the Nazis, the Jews were to blame for the perceived ills of Germany's Weimar Republic. Their alleged catalogue of sins? Among the most heinous and implausible, was that they were behind the Treaty of Versailles, signed under duress after Germany's defeat in the Great War. The Nazis promised to make them disappear. They vowed to drive Rolf's family from their native land.

Rolf and Bert were strangers, whose lives would eventually become entwined. Sport brought them together for an unlikely meeting. Living hundreds of miles apart, living in countries once at war, about to go to war, neither considered such a scenario plausible. As the Nazis took power in Germany's bleak midwinter of 1933, they lived distant, parallel and differing lives. They enjoyed one thing in common – a love of football.

Sport is a release for the masses, football the working man's ballet. It is also prone to tortuous manipulation by malevolent forces. Bert was ambitious. Forget politics. He just wanted to play football for England. Rolf had no desire to play for Nazi Germany, no matter how good he might turn out to be. Just being allowed to play football would be a bonus.

Over in Cheshire, Hitler's rise to power was front-page news. The *Evening Sentinel* drops through the door of the Sproston household. John Sproston picks it up. The front-page splash of Monday, 30 January read, 'HITLER CHANCELLOR OF GERMANY AT LAST!' However, he might need to call fresh elections anyway after a drop in support. Hitler quietly hatched plans to deal with such an inconvenience.

Time to glance at the sport on the *Sentinel* back page. Little of interest, certainly not Chester's 'luck' in the FA Cup fifth round draw. Just how are England getting on down under in the Ashes? John and his boys dedicated most of their spare time to football. But cricket, even in the middle of winter, was an obsession.

England's tour of Australia during 1932/33 was mired in controversy. England secured Test match victories thanks, in part, to controversial bowling tactics. It was just not cricket! There was no score update in the evening newspaper, no need. Instead, the headline ran, 'BODYLINE BOWLING, SECRET MEETING

OF [Australian] BOARD OF CONTROL'. Sproston senior noted that politics appeared to be in danger of embracing sport. Heaven forbid that the same matter happens in football. Hitler also just happened to be hatching his plans for football and sport in general.

Western powers, including Britain, failed to consider the Nazis as a danger to world peace. All originally thought there was little chance of them seizing power. Hitler was not given the Chancellor's job after those summer elections of 1932. The Nazis gained the most seats in parliamentary elections but were kept from power. Instead, an aristocratic Catholic conservative, Franz Von Papen, took the role. His political skills were on a par with a footballer unable to shoot straight.

The Nazi Party's popularity briefly waned, losing millions of votes in yet more German parliamentary elections on 6 November 1932, but they still topped the poll. Remarkably, the hapless Von Papen recommended to President Hindenburg that he appointed Adolf Hitler as Chancellor. Von Papen wrongly calculated that Hitler would fail and relinquish his post. Once democracy put Hitler into power, he made sure it was abolished.

The burning of Germany's parliament building, the Reichstag, on 27 February 1933 served as an excuse for him to suspend the German constitution. He unleashed his storm troopers on a campaign of intimidation and violence; political meetings were broken up. Nazi thugs rounded up social democrats and communists to put them in jail. Yet more parliamentary elections were held on 5 March 1933, just days after the burning of the Reichstag, but these elections were a sham. Millions of Germans still put their faith in their nation's strongman and the cult of Hitler began.

The *Evening Sentinel* helpfully tried to offer its readers in Cheshire and Staffordshire an explanation for the popularity of

Adolf Hitler – a man peddling hate. It argued, 'The secret of Hitler's appeal to the masses lies mainly in his power as a demagogic orator. He addresses his audiences in a voice of thunder and uses the vivid expressions which attract the man in the street.'

Rolf's family descended into despair while Bert's family looked forward to a brighter future. At least Bert thought so. Working as a plumber might soon come to an end as the glamorous life of a professional footballer awaited. Except that Bert never considered that professional football was glamorous. The sport was to be enjoyed, it was a privilege to run out on a Saturday afternoon and entertain the fans. But football was also a way of making a living, albeit a short and perilous one.

Rolf, flicking through his football magazines in Berlin, might beg to differ. His different viewpoint was understandable. There was a certain glamour but just a couple of snags. German athletes competed for honour. Internationally, it was for the honour of the new Reich, the Third Reich. It was for Nazi honour. Football in Germany was also strictly amateur. Nothing to do with the Nazis. They merely adopted a system operating in Germany since imperial times, the days of the Kaiser. Then again, the Nazis cheated the system. Athletes were for them to hire, to exploit. Only Aryan athletes need apply.

Rolf just focused on survival. One by one his family packed their bags and fled Berlin. Escape networks helped the steady stream of refugees fleeing Berlin during the 1930s and it soon became a flood. One no metaphorical plumber was going to stop, not the political flow of humanity.

First, Rolf's dad Adalbert left his family behind in Berlin in December 1935, joining his brother Martin in Rotterdam. He spent life in the Dutch port for a couple of years as one of hundreds of florists, before moving to London. Then, Rolf's younger brother, Hans, left in October 1936. He set sail for the United States from Hamburg with the help of the Kindertransport relief agency. Their mother, Charlotte, planned to join him. After leaving Rolf home alone in Berlin her plans quickly unravelled. The Gestapo locked her up for several weeks in Alexanderplatz. They let her go on the basis that she had a visa to go to Cuba. She flew to England, hoping to board a transatlantic vessel. Her papers were considered invalid, so Rolf's mum remained in England until after the subsequent war, settling near Guildford.

The estranged couple left their young, resourceful and fiercely independent son behind. A once hyperactive kid found plenty to occupy him, not least in avoiding his mother's tormentors from the Gestapo. Rolf planned his own escape from Germany's capital city. He needed help. But who was the Moses-figure to lead him out?

LEEDS UNITED'S RAMBLER

ROLF FRIEDLAND found praying for a saviour to lead him from oppression was easy enough. Just dreamily add to the daily prayers. Finding one turned out to be infinitely more difficult, nothing but a dream. Berlin was no longer home to thousands of its Jewish citizens. They were dispersed across Europe and into corners of the British Empire including Palestine. Many, briefly including Rolf's mum, began to be locked up in Nazi concentration camps. Many were already dead.

'I am going to be reunited with my family,' Rolf told himself on long, lonely nights in the Nazi capital. But how to escape from Berlin, lose the attention of sinister men loyal to Hitler? No point asking a policeman. It would get you arrested. Ask a footballer instead? In the event of England touring Germany, one of its players? A comical idea.

Bert Sproston? The rising star of Leeds United Association Football Club had a simple, almost idyllic, view of life. Put simply, 'Home comforts matter to me, lad. I don't want to ever leave home.' His hometown of Sandbach mattered to him. More specifically and reassuringly for an aspiring athlete, his mother's cooking mattered to him. Healthy living guaranteed in a nation gripped by recession. It was a good enough reason for the young professional footballer to prefer to stay close to home in Cheshire.

Meanwhile, a refugee planned to flee for his life from Berlin to England, one that was eventually to make Tottenham Hotspur FC at White Hart Lane his very own football home. Bert Sproston had little idea as he broke into the England team that he would end up helping the headstrong Berliner. Nor, at the time, did he think he was about to embark on a brief spell at Spurs. Just where Bert might play as a professional footballer and earn a living was effectively beyond his control.

For Bert, let alone Rolf, Britain's capital was an alien land. Leeds United, not for the first nor the last time, found itself in deep financial trouble. Sproston was to be sent on his travels. So just who was this friendly unsung hero of the England football team?

Bertram 'Bert' Sproston was born on 22 June 1915 in the village of Elworth, on the outskirts of Sandbach in Cheshire. As a promising young footballer, he joined local amateur side Elworth Batchelors. On leaving school, he worked as an apprentice to a Sandbach plumber, Mr E. Newall. His brothers were already heading into the building trade. Bert was the youngest of the four and all were promising sportsmen.

Jack Sproston had already played in the Football League with Port Vale. Jack returned to his hometown club Sandbach Ramblers to see out his career in the Cheshire County League. His promising youngest brother Bert was unsurprisingly also picked up by them. His impressive form soon attracted the attention of scouts from Football League clubs.

There were plenty, of course, nearby. Among them, Stoke City and his brother's club Port Vale in the Potteries to the south. The Merseyside giants of Everton and Liverpool, plus Manchester United and Manchester City, to the north. But Sproston headed across the Pennines. His sympathetic plumbing boss gave him permission to go.

Huddersfield Town won the league in the 1920s, champions of England three times in a row under the guidance of legendary manager Herbert Chapman. He went to London, joining Arsenal FC and inspiring them to championship glory. Huddersfield fell from grace but the Terriers remained determinedly ambitious. The club wanted to attract the best young players. Bert Sproston was one of them. He remained a humble and down-to-earth figure for the entirety of his football career. His experience at Huddersfield Town served him well. It was a bruising one.

Bert took up the offer of a trial at Huddersfield during the close season in the summer of 1932 although no contract was on offer. By the time Hitler ended up in power, and snow dusted the Pennine hills, Huddersfield rejected Sproston. Pure coincidence of course. Best for him to keep working, keep hoping. Hope as a prospective professional footballer had not been extinguished.

Bert told of how the episode influenced his football philosophy in the British regional press just a few months before travelling to Germany for the most infamous game in English football history. He wrote in February 1938, 'One of the most striking things about this game of football is the number of "discoveries" made by the various clubs. Week in and week out, during the playing season, one hears or reads of this. So and so, playing in his first match for this or that club, gave a great display – a youngster leaping to fame at one bound. Such stories are almost endless – lads brought into football immediately making good.'

Unfortunately, the Huddersfield management considered that Bert Sproston was too small. It recognised that he was a promising half-back or midfield player. But at 5ft 7in, the Terriers' manager,

Clem Stephenson, considered him to be fragile, not up to the rough and tumble of top-class professional football. Stephenson sent him back to Sandbach Ramblers. Bert returned undaunted across the Pennines. He reckoned it just needed a couple of strokes of luck to succeed.

Firstly, a change of position might help in the rigid tactical system of the day. Secondly, he just needed someone to turn up in Sandbach with a keen eye for his considerable talents. As far as he was concerned, the Huddersfield boss lacked a keen eye.

Sproston later explained in London's defunct newspaper the *Evening News*, 'In my local Sandbach Ramblers teams I was a wing-half, and, being very wilful, insisted on sticking to that position despite advice from several people who knew much better than I did, that I ought to convert myself into a full-back.' Stubbornly he felt that Huddersfield might still offer him a contract as a wing-half or half-back. No contract was forthcoming, although he did have an offer to sign as an amateur for Manchester United in his back pocket. Fate then intervened.

His brother Jack was injured towards the end of the 1932/33 season and Sandbach needed a new full-back. 'There was nothing else for it but to fall one place to the rear,' Sproston remembered of his act of family loyalty. His first game as a defender was against Stalybridge Celtic in an otherwise fairly meaningless Cheshire County League match.

Scouts turning up at the Ramblers' ground still rated Bert, puzzled as much as Bert himself by Huddersfield's rejection. Then, he enjoyed his stroke of luck. The Leeds United manager, Dick Ray, went along to Sandbach with the intention of signing the Stalybridge Celtic player, Charlie Turner – a future Irish international. The young Sandbach right-back also caught his eye, a little sprightlier than the last Sproston he saw playing for the Ramblers.

'It was purely by accident that he learned that this was a different Sproston playing at right-back,' Bert Sproston recalled. 'The Leeds manager thought sufficiently of my play to sign me up at the end of the season. I was then 17 years of age.' Ray also signed Charlie Turner for Leeds United, a productive trip to rural Cheshire.

Ray later said that he was impressed by Sproston's keen tackling and well-judged passing. It reminded him, of course, of another player by the name of Sproston, Bert's much older brother Jack. His career as a full-time professional was over and Bert's professional career was beginning. 'Probably all the time I was growing up, as a wing-back, I was playing more like a full-back: hitting the ball too hard for the liking of my colleagues,' he reflected. 'All the game, I was trying to make good passes and when turning to full-back my experience in the middle line [midfield] probably stood me in good stead.'

Bert snapped up a contract with Leeds United. Football writers considered it a 'wonder' that Huddersfield ever let him go. But, as with many young stars, he was made to wait patiently for his debut. It came for Leeds at Stamford Bridge in a 1-1 draw against Chelsea on 23 December 1933. He played because the regular full-back George Milburn suffered a knee injury. It was an inauspicious debut for Sproston. Chelsea took the lead after he handballed to give away a penalty. But Sproston still impressed the assembled press pack even if they concluded, just like Huddersfield Town, that he was a little on the small side. 'The Sandbach product has a way with him,' observed one Fleet Street writer.

The following season Sproston managed to displace George Milburn as Leeds United's regular right-back. His performance in Leeds' 1-1 draw with Arsenal on 8 September 1934 brought him to national attention. *The People* newspaper revealed to its readers, 'It looks very much as though we shall hear less of the Milburn brothers at back for Leeds this season. The "villain" of the piece is Bert Sproston, a 19-year-old defender, who gave a glorious exhibition against Arsenal. It is not exaggerating matters in the slightest degree to say that Bastin got hardly a smell at the ball, and the extent of the praise is obvious.'

None other than Henry Rose, the doyen of sportswriters back then, recognised young Sproston's potential. Rose's despatch from Berlin four years later chillingly described the England footballers' Nazi salute. His *Daily Express* match report of the game at Highbury in September 1934 noted that a 'boy back' countered the threat of the Gunners' star forward Cliff Bastin. Rose praised 19-year-old Sproston as a 'good un' already. He urged readers to make a note of his name. Little did Rose know but himself, Bastin and Sproston would be reunited in Berlin's Olympiastadion for English football's day of infamy.

Did young Bert take any notice of the thoughts of Henry Rose on his potential as a professional footballer? Doubtful. Bert's view on his sudden elevation to stardom? How to react to critics in the press with notebooks and typewriters? Just keep your feet in football boots firmly on the ground and keep your head on your shoulders.

'I am quite certain, as the result of my experience, that it is easier, in a way, for a young player to make a reputation than it is to live up to it,' he wrote in his syndicated regional newspaper article of February 1938. By this time, he had become an established England international. He illustrated his point by remembering his first game against Arsenal in a tactical analysis of a defender's duties.

'If Leeds United were playing Arsenal, with [Cliff] Bastin at outside-left [left-wing], I should say to myself, "I know that fellow Bastin. He's very good. I mustn't give him an inch of rope." On the other hand, if, instead of Bastin being at outside-left for Arsenal when we played them, they had a youngster of whom I had never heard, I should probably say, "That's all right. He won't do much damage, so I'd better keep an eye on the inside man." The "unknown" is not treated with such deadly seriousness as the known performer. Hence, it is easier for him to make a show and get a good press.'

Wise words and the young man knew the importance of consistently impressing more influential figures than Henry Rose and his mates in the press box. He needed to impress the England selectors. It took some time. A fickle selection ensued – just one cap, then dropped.

It was difficult to keep Bert Sproston out of the England team. Stanley Matthews commented on his old friend in a 2000 autobiography, 'Bert was a down-to-earth lad, who according to the joke of the time, lived on a diet of raw meat and wingers like me.' After chewing up a few rivals, Sproston was selected to make his England debut against Wales at Ninian Park on 17 October 1936.

The *Yorkshire Evening Post* declared that the honour conferred upon him would give great satisfaction to all who knew him. It enthused that he was the best type of professional footballer – keen, studious and taking a pride in personal fitness. 'Besides being clever, he is one of the fastest backs in the league and his ability to recover is a most valuable asset,' the *Yorkshire Evening Post* concluded.

There was just one snag. His Leeds team would miss him in the forthcoming league match against Everton. International breaks did not exist back then. A full league programme went ahead as Wales met England in the home international championship.

Leeds performed quite nicely without Sproston. They beat Everton 3-0. England fared badly despite their young right-back's best efforts. Wales won 2-1. It was their first victory on Welsh soil against England since 1882. The scoreline flattered their opponents. The decision to give six England players their debuts backfired. Sproston spent the game chasing shadows as the Welsh forwards consistently exploited large gaps in the English defence. He had one of his fellow debutants, goalkeeper George Holdcroft of Preston North End, to thank for keeping the score down.

'How are we masters of world football?' Bert dejectedly wondered. 'We lost to a rugby nation.' He hoped to keep his place for the following international against Ireland at Stoke City's Victoria Ground. Ideal for his mum in nearby Sandbach to come and watch him. Unfortunately, the selectors dropped him after watching him in an England shirt just once. Arsenal's George Male reclaimed his place. Worse still, the England selectors made Male captain.

The England goalkeeper Holdcroft, who was born in the Potteries and began his career at Port Vale, kept his place. Unsurprisingly, so too did another England debutant, Stoke City's centre-forward Freddie Steele. But there was to be no short trip to Stoke for Bert Sproston's mum to see her son play for England.

Indeed, he struggled to win his place back. England went on a tour of Scandinavia, a trip English football critics failed to take seriously. Sproston missed the tour, an international career on hold for one of the country's most promising players. Perhaps the FA's selectors took umbrage at the precocious young star willingly offering his views in the press on how football ought to be played.

Stanley Matthews reflected that his friend Bert considered himself to be a man of limited education. It is true that Sproston left school at 14 years old. But, just like Matthews, he grew into an articulate advocate for his sport and newspapers regularly carried his thoughts on the game.

Just by way of controversy or honest opinion, he thought that strikers were a little overrated. He felt that defenders were undervalued – absolute heresy for many football fans of any era.

'Discussions about the most difficult position to fill on the football field are very popular among football players and followers and cause many hours of amusement,' Sproston began. 'Seldom do they lead to any definite decision, because in the case of every position it is possible to produce arguments to prove that it is the most exacting of all. Human nature usually sees to it that every player thinks his own position the hardest.'

Rather cheekily Sproston singled out a full-back, 'who has represented this country many times in recent years', for polite criticism. How dare he suggest that it is much harder to be a forward than a defender? Sproston did not name him but a quick flick through the archive shows that George Male of Arsenal was never slow in putting his view forward. He usually did so just like Sproston in syndicated columns for the regional press.

Sproston threatened Male's spot as England's regular right-back. Effectively calling out a favourite of the perennial league champions for his views on the national game hardly endeared Sproston to the football establishment. This included some Fleet Street correspondents who had never played the game at top-class domestic or international level. A source of irritation to him. He was unaware at the time but he would experience first-hand the disdain for George Male's Arsenal from fans of rival London clubs, especially Tottenham Hotspur.

Despite his impressive league form, Sproston needed to bide his time before reclaiming his England place, only to end up playing in one of his country's most controversial games. England's leading clubs admired him, even if the England selectors ignored him. Leeds United's perilous finances put him firmly in the spotlight. Their directors felt they had no choice but to sell their best players. In fairness, the club had resisted offers for their fine young England international full-back, albeit for the time being a one-cap wonder.

Oddly, one of those clubs just happened to be Arsenal. Male suffered a knee injury, keeping him out of the Gunners' team for several weeks. Leeds rejected their attempt to sign Sproston as part of a deal to sign Arsenal's centre-forward Jimmy Dunne. The Irishman had lost his place to Ted Drake. Arsenal's manager George Allison, if not the England international selectors, appeared to appreciate Sproston's attributes. Male remained at Arsenal. Sproston remained at Leeds. But Male's injury meant the possibility of the Leeds full-back winning his England place back.

On a blustery autumnal night in Glasgow, Bert sat in the dressing room at Ibrox proudly clutching a piece of paper. It was a telegram from the chairman of Sandbach town council. Mr J.H. Jennings congratulated this son of Sandbach on being picked to play for England against Scotland on 22 September 1937. It was good of Jennings to contact him. Naturally, the Sandbach councillor even made sure to inform the *Crewe Chronicle* of his gesture.

For Sproston, it was his first encounter with a politician dabbling in the world of football. Councillor Jennings's note almost also certainly provoked a wry smile. Unfortunately, the hapless local politician appeared to know little about football. Bert was making an international debut but only of sorts. It was technically not for England. The FA selectors had yet to give him his place back in the national team. Instead, he was picked for the English league to play the Scottish league at the home of Rangers Football Club. It was still an honour. Sadly, the match went badly the Scots won 1-0.

Charles Buchan, a former England international and by then one of sports journalism's more opinionated and vociferous critics, lambasted the English league team. He did spare Sproston. Buchan wrote in the *News Chronicle* on 23 September 1937, 'There were enough gaps in the ranks for a regiment of soldiers to pass through.'

Buchan went further, 'Lack of understanding threw a lot of work on the England rearguard, but Sproston and [Sam] Barkas stood firm, and this pair kept the opposing forwards at a safe distance from [goalkeeper Vic] Woodley. Sproston's pace, too, was an asset and the calculated kicking of Barkas started many attacks. No fault could be placed on the English rearguard.' So, could Bert look forward to a return to the full England team? Well, not just yet.

Another appearance for the English league team, this time against the Irish league, failed to win over the selectors. The English won 3-0 at Blackpool's Bloomfield Road ground. The *Daily Mirror* commented that there were few chances of judging the English defence and accused Sproston and company of taking a few liberties in what was a glorified exhibition game. Cue another glorified exhibition game for the benefit of England's football selectors.

In a nod to the amateur era, the FA staged a 'probables' versus 'possibles' game at Goodison Park. Charles Buchan implausibly moaned that the match failed to attract Merseyside soccer fans in their tens of thousands. Just 8,000 turned up on 13 October 1937 to witness a 1-1 draw. After the game, the FA selectors met in the Everton FC boardroom. It took them 20 minutes to pick the team. Bert Sproston was back. Indeed, he briefly became an automatic choice. Northern football correspondents celebrated his reinstatement. Their London-based colleagues from Fleet Street were less sure.

The *Manchester Evening News* noted that the people of Cheshire and its county league would be taking special pride. It declared him to be the best young back in English league football, a finely built player with speed to match that of any flying winger and possessing great positional play. His restoration to the England line-up, this time for a long-term spell, meant yet more transfer interest. Again, Leeds United resisted.

England beat Ireland 5-1 on 23 October 1937 in Belfast, followed by a 2-1 victory over Wales at Ayresome Park in Middlesbrough on 17 November 1937. White Hart Lane staged England's final international of the year. England beat Czechoslovakia 5-4 in a game as thrilling as the scoreline suggested.

Sproston enjoyed his partnership down the right wing with Stanley Matthews. But given England conceded a record number of goals on home soil to a continental side, Sproston's place came under pressure. Fleet Street football correspondents called for the return of Arsenal's Male. They argued that once Male was restored to fitness, there was no room for Sproston. Male must play against Scotland at Wembley.

The selectors disagreed. They decided to remain loyal to Leeds United's young full-back. Sproston was in peak form for club and country. His first league goal came at Molineux on 5 March 1938 in a 1-1 draw with Wolves, a free kick from 16 yards sailing well clear of the goalkeeper. The *Yorkshire Post* expressed relief that the England selectors remained loyal to the Leeds right-back. 'Sproston undoubtedly deserves his place, and the many admirers of the Leeds United back will be glad that he has been retained,' the *Yorkshire Post* told its Leeds-supporting readers.

England suffered an embarrassing 1-0 defeat to Scotland at Wembley on 9 April 1938 – England's first defeat to the Scots at Wembley in a decade. It failed to panic the selectors into wholesale changes to the team. England deserved to lose by more. But Sproston kept his place at right-back. His performance drew grudging praise from Scottish football writers at Wembley. He lacked 'personality' but was among the better England performers. His opposite number, Brentford's left-winger, Bobby Reid, was dismissed as lacking in Scottish national temperament. Thanks to Sproston he was 'broken up and jittery'.

Stan Cullis, the centre-half, lost out and was blamed for Scotland's winning goal as Blackpool's centre-forward Frank O'Donnell outjumped him to set up the winning goal. Tommy Walker scored with a rasping shot past Vic Woodley. O'Donnell was described as 'immense'. Paul Irwin of *Reynolds News* wrote, 'To my mind, the game turned on Frank O'Donnell's early duels with Stan Cullis. The Scot was beating the England centre-half with ease.' Cullis suffered a dent to his reputation. He travelled to Europe as a reserve. He was not picked to play against Germany, counted out long before the touring England team reached Berlin.

One other decision emerged from the meeting of the FA's England selectors. They agreed to stage a football match between England and a Rest of Europe team on Wednesday, 26 October 1938. The venue for what they called an 'attraction', as part of the

FA's 75th anniversary celebrations, was yet to be decided. The fixture certainly attracted the attention of a Jewish teenager in Berlin. Rolf Friedland eagerly looked forward to England's arrival in Berlin. As an obsessive sports fan with attention to detail, he also noted in his diary the invitation for Europe's best players, including some from Germany, to go to England. Neither Rolf nor Bert quite appreciated the personal significance of this testimonial game at the time. But it did give Rolf the germ of an idea.

Bert Sproston was on his way for the fateful game against Germany – a football match overshadowed by political games. Little did Bert know as he set off on the boat train in early May 1938, that amid controversy he was about to become English football's greatest unsung hero – nothing to do with his physical strength, speed, timing of a tackle and stroking of a football. It was all down to basic human decency, a man in touch with his humanity.

FORBIDDEN GAMES

OVER IN Berlin, Rolf Friedland waited patiently for a saviour. Still, he allowed himself a mild and reflective moment of religious fervour as he rested from his latest sporting endeavours. The England football team were on their way to Berlin, presenting an opportunity to watch the creators of association football. Not only that but the self-confessed masters of the beautiful game.

As his mind rambled out of control, he mused to himself that perhaps, a sports star might well be his saviour, at least an inspiration? Ridiculous but why not? 'Joseph Goebbels's gob' informed him of the England football team's impending arrival. Goebbels's gob? More of that later.

Scraping around for a living remained a priority and odd jobs helped. They did so even if it meant hiding his religious and racial background. Few employers would want to hire him if they knew he was Jewish. Some Jewish businesses, a rapidly declining number, remained open. A printing firm, Mannes and Company, hired Rolf as an apprentice at the age of 15, allowing him to make a sparse living.

Football also provided a novel source of scant funding. A scattering of Jewish football clubs still operated throughout Berlin. The Nazis took their time in shutting them all down. Those clubs were willing to offer token payments to the most promising teenage players. Rolf just happened to be one and he joined the Berliner Sport Gemeinschaft. He would turn out for anyone caring to pick him, provided they left cash in his boots; a few pfennigs would do.

Why bother to stick with German football's tradition of amateurism with the country under the grip of the Nazis? The cash given to him helped to supplement his wages from the printers. He just turned up at a recreation ground in the hope of being offered a game, plus the cash to pay for his supper. It also satisfied a rebellious and mischievous streak.

Sport mattered to both Bert and Rolf – all sport. Bert, along with his brothers, developed their love of cricket. For all the crushing snobbery at elite level of England's national summer game, cricket remained a working-class sport enjoyed by the northern English masses. The Sprostons maintained their links with Sandbach Cricket Club – not just enthusiastic but useful players in Cheshire, a minor cricket county. Weekend cricket in the North Staffordshire and South Cheshire League was fiercely competitive and remains so.

Rolf embraced one of Berlin's unashamedly elitist sports. Messing about on lakes and rivers suited the conventional German appreciation of sport. Germans promoted pure athletic disciplines, *Turnen* or *Gymnastik*. This appeared threatened by the growth of the working-class sport of football. It was even dismissed by critics as the 'English disease'. Regional sports associations popped up everywhere in Germany, beginning arguably with the German cricket and football association of Berlin in 1881. Forget cricket, football and rowing caught the sporting imagination of a German teenager.

He loved the competitive freedom of going on the water. Rowing and canoeing, against all logic given the prevailing climate, managed to thrive as sports among Berlin's persecuted Jewish community during the 1930s. The Nazis ignored the growth of Jewish clubs in what the English might consider a distinctly posh boys' sport. Tim Kock wrote in 2015 for the UK rowing website *Hear the Boat Sing* about the *Jüdischer Ruder-Clubs* of Nazi Germany, 'That they existed at all before 1933 is interesting; that they continued to exist (and for a time grow) in the first five years of Nazi rule, 1933–38, is difficult to comprehend.'

Handball also proved popular among Jewish youths as the Nazis turned a blind eye to their sports clubs. Then again, they needed to be of strictly sectarian nature. They were not allowed to join any other clubs. Teenage Jews played their sport at the unofficial *sportplatz* in the Berlin Grunewald. It was a rare concession, a minor one.

The clue to the Nazis easing up on their clampdown on Jews competing in sport quite possibly lay with the staging of the Olympics, both the Winter Games at Garmisch-Partenkirchen in February 1936 and the Summer Games in Berlin of August 1936. Hitler had dismissed the proud Olympic movement in predictable racist rhetoric as a 'plot by Freemasons and Jews'. But his propaganda minister, Joseph Goebbels, quickly spotted the advantages of staging an Olympics. There was no complaints from genuine German sports fans such as Rolf, even if Dr Goebbels's immense interest might be unwelcome.

The 1936 Olympics in Berlin more famously served as an example of the Nazis trying to use sport as a tool to promote a modern, even tolerant, Germany. It was modern but it was certainly not tolerant. The Nazis pretended otherwise. Rolf on his travels through his home city would have noted a temporary transformation during those Games.

Open hostility to Rolf's faith, creed and race disappeared. *Juden Unerwünscht'* (Jews unwanted or not welcome) signs, seen all over Germany since Hitler came to power, were removed from Berlin's hotels, restaurants, bars and other public places. Anyone deemed 'undesirable', those people likely to embarrass the Nazis, were rounded up and locked up, kept out of sight from tourists and inquisitive foreign journalists. Rolf already knew it was best to keep a low profile, ignore provocation and settle for a quiet life.

Not everyone, of course, escaped unwarranted attention. Not just Jews, but the Roma/Sinti population, political opponents and even some vocal members of the Roman Catholic Church. Hitler was Catholic by birth. A lapsed Catholic might be a generous description of his irreligious views. On just one infamous day, 16 July 1936, more than 800 Roma/Sinti were detained by police and frog-marched to a camp on the outskirts of Berlin. The Nazis had not just built an Olympic village for athletes; they built a detention centre for a race of people they considered to be inferior.

As for Berlin's Jewish population, Hitler's notorious elite army corps, the SS, were ordered to refrain from taking any action against them. For once, they were to be left alone. However, any foreign journalist, wanting to speak to Jewish leaders and gain an insight into life under the Nazis, had to go to the Gestapo for permission. From that point onwards, the secret police closely monitored those journalists for the duration of the Games. Just as an added measure, another act of deceit, the anti-Semitic publication *Der Stürmer* was absent from newsstands. It would be back in circulation after the Games.

Rolf was unaware of another Jewish teenager embracing sport as welcome relief, his future wife Eva. 'One last ray of sunshine on the scene of Nazi Germany was the event of the Olympic Games of 1936,' Eva recalled. 'Berlin in 1936 once again sparkled and Berliners with it. The anti-Jewish campaign had been reduced to impress the foreign visitors, and one was free to come and go and the air was warm and fresh. I danced whenever possible.'

She also credited her 'cool head' for recognising that the Nazis were trying to con the international community during the 1936 Olympic Summer Games. Rolf felt the same. Their brief period of freedom quickly ended. 'I did not overlook the facts that the Nazi campaign was growing again after the Olympic Games, and the great advice of friends was: Get out of Germany before a war will start,' she wrote.

'Anyone who may have studied the social impact on Jewish life in Germany will know that by now the signs were up anywhere *Juden Unerwünscht,* Jews not wanted, be it in restaurants or theatres, or hotels. We had in the community the *Jüdischer Kultur bund,* the Jewish cultural centre, and it was there that one now went for films, concert, or theatre. The writing was on literally every wall. Jews out!'

The 1936 Summer Olympic Games were originally awarded by the IOC to Berlin before the Nazis took power. IOC members rejected the favourites, Rome, partly and ironically on the basis that Italy was a fascist state. The German fascist state might have done the IOC a favour if the Nazis declined the offer to go ahead with the staging of the Games. They did not.

Such were Goebbels's powers of persuasion, he somehow managed to convince his sceptical Führer of international sport's value. The Nazis wanted to give the impression that they were behaving themselves on the sports field, despite growing evidence to the contrary.

Jesse Owens managed to ruin Goebbels's propaganda triumph at the Berlin Olympics. The African American superstar sprinter inspired Rolf. Nothing gave him greater pleasure than being sat in Berlin's Olympiastadion as Owens booked his place in history – the man responsible for destroying the myth of Aryan superiority. In doing so, Owens inspired millions of others.

For Rolf, the Nazis' political games at the Olympics were impossible to ignore. Then again, he thought it best just to appreciate the sport on offer – the skill, the guile, grace and pure athleticism of some of the world's greatest sports stars. For him it was a bonus to witness the political implications – he had looked on admiringly from the Olympiastadion's vast stands as Jesse Owens spoiled the Nazis' propaganda party. The sight of Owens destroying the myth of Aryan superiority at the Berlin Olympics in August 1936 provided fond memories.

Neither Rolf nor his future wife, Eva, needed reminders of the Nazis' cynicism and disdain for sport, especially the involvement of non-Aryan athletes. Football was a key example. The German football association, Deutscher Fußball-Bund (DFB) was openly racist, even prior to the Nazis taking power. Football clubs needed no missives from the Nazis to boot out Jewish members. They already began doing so. It became formal policy soon after the Reichstag burned down.

Rolf, as did so many of his mates, eagerly awaited the German football magazine *Der Kicker* to drop through his front door's letterbox. On 19 April 1933, he noted an appallingly racist advertisement, taken out by the DFB in *Der Kicker,* a publication set up by Jewish businessmen – chief among them, one of its founders Walther Bensemann.

It stated that 'members of the Jewish race, and persons who turned out to be followers of the Marxist movement, are deemed unacceptable'. It also urged clubs 'to initiate appropriate measures, if they have not yet been taken'. In other words, expel any Jewish members. Football played a minor part in the Olympics, especially considering the decision to exclude professionals. It was not even included for the Los Angeles Olympics of 1932, a decision that left FIFA feeling free to create the World Cup in 1930.

No German institutions were safe from the Nazis, especially those devoted to sport. As a warning, the Nazi Party newspaper, *Völkischer Beobachter,* declared when Germany won the right to stage the 1936 Olympics, 'The next Olympic Games will take place in Berlin. Blacks must be excluded. We demand it.' It later moderated its racist tone on the orders of the Nazi hierarchy, chief among them Hitler's propaganda minister Joseph Goebbels. These men were fearful of losing their prized Olympic propaganda tool once they took power.

Until then, sport simply served as a means of just maintaining military fitness for Hitler and his henchman. Hitler's rambling polemic *Mein Kampf* hardly serves as a guidebook to sport. But among its hate-filled pages, sport does feature, albeit in less than enthusiastic terms. There was no nod to Olympian or Corinthian ideals. The acknowledgment of sport was simply utilitarian. Hitler wrote, 'Not a day should go by in which the young man does not receive one hour of physical training in the morning and one hour in the afternoon, covering every type of sport and gymnastics.'

Team sport played no part and it certainly was not for fun. His notorious *Sturmabteilung* (SA), the storm troopers or Brownshirts, were registered with the Weimar Republic's police as a sports association. Apart from boxing and gymnastics, their members shunned conventional sport. The only team sport the SA went near to practising just happened to be street brawls. These were far more vicious than even football hooligans managed decades later. Hitler declared, 'A decayed body is not made the least more aesthetic by a brilliant mind, indeed the highest intellectual training could not be justified if its bearers were at the same time physically degenerate and crippled, weak-willed, wavering and cowardly individuals.'

Physical fitness mattered. Building it up simply to play football rather than terrify political opponents was of zero value. The Nazis firmly believed in *Wehrsport* (military sport) but soon realised, due to Goebbels, that it might just have other uses.

The British ambassador to Berlin, Sir Eric Phipps, warned his Whitehall bosses in December 1934, 'The impression left by the summer and autumn is one of incessant marching and drilling. It is evident to any foreign observer that the German people, with their innate love of discipline and military training, are revelling in their new freedom. Even the demonstrations of the labour front and the peasant rallies seem to the outsider to be mainly military parades. We have to face the fact that, while other countries enjoy playing football or sipping coffee under trees, German youth is happiest at playing soldiers, and German manhood is happiest on the barrack square.'

Nazis administered German sport under the German Reich's Committee for Physical Exercise *Deutscher Reichsbund für Leibesübungen* (DRL). It served as an umbrella organisation for all sports federations and individual clubs. Sir Eric Phipps made casual, if not xenophobic observations of the German people and their attitude to sport. The Nazis formalised them.

Prior to the Berlin Olympics, the Nazis slowly but surely exerted their control over the German population, especially those opposed to them but then willing to fall for their doctrine. The Nazis eventually formed an organisation called, without a trace of irony, 'Strength through Joy' or in German *Kraft Freudemer*. Only Teutonic or Aryan strength mattered – very little room for joy.

Hitler appointed Hans von Tschammer und Osten as its *Reichssportkommissar*, later termed his *Reichssportführer*. Von Tschammer und Osten declared, 'German sports are for Aryans. German youth leadership is Aryans only, and not for Jews.' An SA thug and Nazi loyalist, he appeared ideal for the role. Unfortunately, Von Tschammer und Osten knew next to nothing about sport. Germany's football association, the DFB, remained in place but was relegated to a subsidiary body of the DRL. Teenage football fell under the control of the Hitler Youth.

In a sense, of course, it was not necessary for the Nazis to take over the DFB. Nazifying the German football association was never a problem. The infamous racist advert in *Der Kicker* illustrated the point. German sports organisations, especially individual football clubs, quite happily joined the anti-Semitic frenzy. Even before Hitler became the German Chancellor there was a disturbing trend. One by one, German sports federations began excluding Jews.

The Nazis tried to keep this quiet, aware of the importance of the forthcoming Berlin Olympics and the growing threat of a boycott. Exclusively Jewish sports clubs remained in operation but they were excluded from mainstream competition. Unfortunately for the Nazis, the governors of German football scuppered any attempts to suppress details of their multitude of sins. It made little difference.

The British football associations co-operated with the DFB throughout the 1930s, something they refused to do in the immediate aftermath of the Great War. In the spirit of building friendship between the British and German people, the FA lifted its boycott. It saw no reason to reinstate it once Hitler took power, despite evidence of racial discrimination in German football.

FA bosses also failed to notice the German dictator's utilitarian attitude to sport. It was hardly in the old Corinthian spirit so beloved of the English public schoolboys, who founded the sport of association football. It was also no secret. On 14 December 1933, Hitler outlined his bleak vision for sport.

Confirming he had agreed to the building of an Olympic stadium for the 1936 Berlin Olympics, Hitler commented, 'Buildings alone are not sufficient to guarantee that German sports are accorded a position in the international competitions which corresponds to the world prestige of our nation. Much more significant is the unified, committed will of the nation to choose the best competitors out of all Germany's *Gaue* [Nazi administrative district] and to train and steel them so that we may pass the forthcoming competition with honours. A no less important task is the sustained and lasting attention to physical exercise in the entire German *Volk* [people] as one of the most important cultural assets of the National Socialist state. We will make of this a permanent basis for the spirit of the new Germany in the physical strength of its *Volk*.'

So much for any notion of sporting joy. Athletes were nothing more than state assets. Even Soviet leaders with their doped athletes of the Cold War years were not so publicly explicit. Hitler's *Reichssportführer*, Von Tschammer, worked to ensure the successful domination of German sport on the world stage. Hitler added, 'I ask all organisations, official bodies, etc., to grant him every possible support and encouragement.'

By 14 March 1935, Hitler issued another sporting missive: this time officially defining sport as a means of aiding the military. Just prior to the introduction of conscription in Germany, it read,

'The new state requires a robust, hardy race. Our superior training of the spirit must be accompanied and reinforced by an aggressive training of the body by means of simple, useful, and natural physical exercises. In order to give added impetus and direction to the efforts of our youth, I am establishing the award of the SA sports badge for the entire SA and all of its former sections; it is to be awarded upon completion of a conscientiously discharged period of training when an achievement test has been passed. In order to lend a more conscious expression to the cultivation of military spirit (*wehrhafter Geist*) in every area of the German *Volk*, I further direct that this SA sports badge may also be acquired and worn by non-members of the movement insofar as they fulfil, within a racial and superior sense, the National Socialist requirements.'

After finishing his odd jobs on 4 December 1935, Rolf sat glued to the radio with commentary of England's game against Germany. England easily won at Tottenham Hotspur's White Hart Lane ground 3-0. It brought rare cheer to the Friedland household. Rolf's dad was already packing his bags to escape the Nazis. Football relieved the gloom and patriotic norms disappeared. German Jews no longer wanted to support Germany. Certainly not while the country was under Nazi rule. Certainly not Rolf Friedland.

Some British ministers realised even prior to kick-off that the Nazis were cynical in their manipulation of sport. None, of course, publicly admitted as much. They had resisted calls for England's game against Germany at White Hart Lane to be called off. Spurs traditionally enjoyed support from London's Jewish community. They vehemently opposed the staging of the game along with the Labour and trade union movement.

Privately, the then Home Secretary, Sir John Simon, expressed doubts. He informed cabinet members in a now declassified paper, 'There seems to me to be strong reason to believe that it [The England versus Germany international match] is really a piece of political propaganda in the interests of the Nazis.' Sir John concluded as an estimated 10,000 German fans were on their way to London, 'Why should we approve of this Nazi invasion?' Sir John asked the foreign secretary, Sir Samuel Hoare, for support. None was forthcoming so the controversial fixture went ahead. Would England go to Berlin to play Germany? Much to Rolf's delight, the answer was yes. 'Goebbels's gob' gave him the answer.

Young Friedland sat alone in his Berlin flat, cleaning his precious football boots. The wireless crackled away in the background. His family kindly and metaphorically left behind what was nicknamed 'Goebbels's gob', not the most welcome of gifts. Hitler's propaganda minister ordered the construction of millions of cheap radio sets, the *Volksempfänger*, to go into German homes. They were a functional and affordable source of entertainment for the working classes and a tool of the news for the German ruling class. Goebbels believed in the power of radio.

Rolf wrestled with his football boots' blunted studs and banged out the caked mud. Just occasionally he hammered them against the stone floor in frustration. It would soon need cleaning too. He paid no attention to the radio, just focused on scraping off the mud covering his boots. It was late autumn and had been turning into yet another long, hard, wet and muddy season. Then the radio broadcast attracted his attention.

For once, the radio ramblings cheered Rolf. The news of an Anglo-German football match came through on 16 November

1937. The English FA had agreed that the national team would travel to Berlin in May 1938 to play Germany. Oddly, this piece of news had apparently failed to reach the ears of British ministers and civil servants in Whitehall.

The FA and DFB finalised arrangements for the game in Berlin during November 1937. They did so as England played Czechoslovakia for the last time in a while. Concerns over the future of Czechoslovakia were consuming diplomatic minds by the time England's footballers arrived in Berlin. England beat Czechoslovakia 5-4 at White Hart Lane on 1 December 1937, Stanley Matthews scoring a hat-trick.

Rolf, as he admired his battered and muddied football boots, pondered on the possibility of going to see the great Matthews. What a chance to watch another sporting icon in action. It was, of course, a lifetime privilege to witness Jesse Owens perform his legendary feats at the Berlin Olympics. Now the chance to see whether England's star man was as good as his admirers made out. Rolf had hardly heard of any of the other England players, not least a promising defender from Leeds United by the name of Bert Sproston.

But was the staging of yet another high-profile sports event just another Nazi propaganda stunt? The British were admired for bringing association football, or in German *Fußball,* to the world. Cricket was the sport of the British Empire, not so football, whether rugby or soccer. Unfortunately, at the height of empire, the British nation's diplomatic skills were on the wane, at least the ability to spot a rogue, evil regime.

Many foreign powers, the British and Americans among them, left the Nazis' Olympic Games in Berlin of 1936 feeling distinctly impressed. They ignored the Nazification of sport, the pursuit of Aryan glorification and superiority. Sporting links to Nazi Germany were actively encouraged against the backdrop of appeasement.

As autumn gave way to winter in mid-November 1937, the radio enthusiastically welcomed another sporting propaganda opportunity. Rolf, even in his tender youth, recognised the proposed Anglo-German football match as such. Perhaps not on an Olympic scale, but still significant. He took less notice of news of the visit of English aristocrat Lord Halifax to Berlin. Halifax was off to a sports exhibition, then tea with Hitler in Bavaria. Young Rolf surmised that the naive and arrogant British foreign minister was wasting his time. Hitler wanted war. Quite oddly, a game of football between Germany and England came first – a substitute for war.

The radio propaganda promised a warm welcome for the fathers of football. Rolf paused from scrubbing his football boots and a flight of fancy crossed his mind. The broadcast, interspersed with military music, became hypnotic. Rolf fell almost into a trance, not one to necessarily meet the approval of the Nazis. A mad idea flashed across his mind. Maybe, there just might be a personal opportunity. 'How to gain a visa for a trip to England?' he kept asking himself. A one-way trip to England; just don't bother to tell anyone of the true purpose. No better way than meeting an Englishman in Berlin. Better still, engineer a meeting with an England football star.

The international friendly planned for the spring at Berlin's Olympiastadion gave him the opportunity. Rolf went back to scrubbing his muddy boots. Hitler wanted to use a football match for propaganda purposes. A teenager alone in Berlin planned to use it for an escape. He had six months to plan his audacious bid for freedom. Prepare to welcome the England football team to Berlin. Give them a personal surprise. Ask one of them to support an application for asylum in the UK.

TEA WITH HITLER

A COUPLE of smartly dressed English tourists left their plush hotel in Berlin for an enjoyable stroll in the spring sunshine. They paused outside a cafe. An enthusiastic waiter greeted them. '*Guten Tag.*' One of them answers 'allo!' awkwardly in English. 'Ah. Hello, gentlemen. Englanders? You are here from England? You are here for the match tomorrow?' He failed to recognise them. One was the England international defender Bert Sproston, the other one of the world's most famous footballers, Stanley Matthews.

Both cheerfully acknowledged that they were in Berlin for the game, Germany versus England at Berlin's Olympiastadion. More than 100,000 spectators would fill the vast arena. For the game between Germany and the English inventors of football, it could have been sold out four times over. Tens of thousands of German football fans were descending on Berlin. Many arrived in the capital on chartered trains from all over Germany. Travel costs were subsidised by the Nazi government. English football fans were a rarity. Only a select few fans travelled abroad to support England for any fixture, let alone one held in a totalitarian country.

The waiter was intrigued by his customers. Much to Matthews's chagrin, Hollywood film stars were instantly recognisable. They earned large pay cheques requisite with their talent, just as importantly fame. International footballers were not instantly recognisable, not outside their home countries. They also earned a relative pittance. German footballers were not even paid. As mentioned earlier, the Nazis stuck to the decades-old German principles of amateurism. It was something of a sham.

Sproston attempted a joke; laughed as he told the waiter that they hoped to get a game. They even brought their boots, just in case. Then he offered his hand in a further greeting, 'I am Bert, Bert Sproston.' The puzzled waiter hesitated. The name was vaguely familiar. He then looked across to Sproston's friend. 'And I suppose you are Stanley Matthews?' The three of them laughed. At least he had heard of them, even if he failed to recognise them.

The waiter remained blissfully unaware that he was entertaining celebrity guests; at least the best on offer from England in 1930s Berlin. Sproston asked the friendly English-speaking waiter for a pot of tea. As the waiter went to fetch a brew for his guests, Sproston teased Matthews.

'Pot of tea Stan, but no cups from Stoke-on-Trent?' He chortled as Matthews struggled to raise a smile. The pair of them settled down, basking in the sunshine. Just the odd car, van and tram rumbled by.

Suddenly, the pair heard the growing roars of crowds nearby. To a couple of experienced professional footballers, the din was reminiscent of a matchday. They looked puzzled as the pavement was engulfed by fans, but not football supporters who might recognise them. In an instant, men, women and children gathered outside the cafe, lining the street and enthusiastically waving their red, black and white Nazi flags. The cheering slowly competed with the roar of motorbike and car engines.

Sproston and Matthews quizzically looked at each other as the noise intensified, both the roar of the vehicles and cheers of a fanatical crowd. Customers inside the cafe headed for the door, anxious to join the cheering throng. The waiter came out with his tray and briefly joined the crowd. The roars, the euphoria subsided. The whir of engines disappeared into the distance.

Matthews piped up. 'Sounds like some grand fromage has just passed by, Bert.' Just a shrug of the shoulders from his friend. 'We're in Germany, not France, Stan,' he dismissively replied. 'Yes, it must be someone of importance judging by the rumpus.'

A tall man standing by the door spotted the English pair. He, just like the waiter, failed to recognise them. His knowledge of English was good. He informed them, 'You underestimate the importance of the occasion, gentlemen. This was our beloved Führer gracing us with his presence.' The waiter approached them with his pot of tea, a jug of milk and a huge smile across his face. He too overheard the comments of his guests. It was as if Hitler was God.

Matthews and Sproston nodded warily before the waiter walked off, a spring in his step after paying homage to his Führer. 'Hitler dinna stay for long Bert,' Matthews commented while stifling a laugh. He paused before picking up his teacup and sighed. There was unwelcome news to share with his friend.

'According to the skipper, the British ambassador here in Berlin wants us to salute Hitler before kick-off at tomorrow's match. Mark of respect apparently,' Matthews told him. Sproston was briefly startled. 'You what?' Matthews commented that he believed that they had no choice. Then again, they did not even know if Hitler would turn up. He was hardly noted as a fan of football. Quite the opposite. Bert pondered for a moment, staring out into the distance. He then asked whether Matthews knew the view of the FA boss, Stanley Rous. 'Yes, that pompous old ref,' Matthews wryly responded, 'met the ambassador for dinner last night.' Quite a meeting.

The British ambassador to Berlin, Sir Nevile Henderson, just happened to be a crushing snob, even by the standards of the day. Dealing with a bunch of footballers was beneath him. He enjoyed a habit of wearing an Old Etonian cricket tie. In those times, he saw it as enough to put grammar schoolboy Rous in his lowly place. Members of Henderson's social class were unimpressed by the FA boss. Men such as Henderson preferred cricket to any code of football – the gentlemen's game played by hooligans.

A future British prime minister, Harold MacMillan, later described Henderson's appointment as the UK's ambassador to Berlin as a 'complete disaster'. He was, 'hysterical, self-opinionated and unreliable'. Never more so than on the eve of an eagerly anticipated football match between England and Germany.

Henderson simply wanted to focus on how to win friends and attempt to influence one of the most evil regimes in history. Of course, cricket fan Henderson still wanted England to win the football match. Bert Sproston just happened to be a better cricketer than Henderson could ever dream of. So too were many of his team-mates in the England football team. Just to stretch a metaphor, a little awkward googly was dreamt up for them by the British establishment. Henderson asked Rous to deliver it.

The British ambassador to Berlin advised the FA to ask the players to make the Nazi salute. It was more of a demand than a polite suggestion. He put it to Rous and the former England international, Charles Wreford-Brown, who was nominally put in charge of the England team. Sir Stanley Rous, who later became president of FIFA, claimed in his 1978 autobiography *Football*

Worlds, A Lifetime in Sport that the Nazi salute was merely a matter of courtesy. According to Rous, Henderson told them, 'When I go to see Herr Hitler, I give him the Nazi salute because that is the normal courtesy expected. It carries no hint of approval of anything Hitler or his regime may do. And if I do it, why should you or your team object?' It appeared that the FA secretary had no problem with such a high-handed and dismissive view.

Maybe Rous never came across the diplomatic gossip. For the past few weeks, the FA had come under pressure from the British government to comply with its demands. Ministers trumped the mantra that politics had nothing to do with sport – at least they did so publicly.

Quite slowly throughout the 1930s, the British came to realise the value of sport as a tool of diplomatic soft power. The Nazis needed no persuading. The British approach just happened to be bizarre. Britain placed the onus on teams and individual athletes to demonstrate on their travels that they were jolly good chaps. British values of courtesy and fair play mattered. These were at the core of British sport, hence the excuse to be offered that giving the Nazi salute might just be a matter of courtesy.

The FA boss, Sir Stanley Rous, admitted that Henderson consistently warned of the dangers posed by sporting links with Nazi Germany. He wanted them to stop. What was the Nazi aim? According to Henderson, they were looking for easy victories to boost the idea that the regime had produced a 'super-race'. Rous dismissed such an idea as nonsense. There was zero chance of easy victories against England, the masters of the world game of football. It never dawned on the hapless English administrator that the Nazis might still achieve their propaganda victory by ordering England's footballers to make a Hitler salute.

Foreign Office officials had panicked just before the England team set off for Berlin. Oddly, they had needed prompting. Whitehall ministers and mandarins feigned surprise at the timing of this sports fixture. The publisher, Harvey V. Usill, contacted his friend, Sir Stephen Gaselee, at the Foreign Office. He specifically warned him that the impending clash between Germany and England in Berlin's Olympic Stadium was more than just a football match to the Nazis. Usill's company, Evans Brothers, constantly worked with the FA to produce football titles, along with its regular portfolio of children's and educational books. In carrying out his work, especially compiling the *Year Book of Education*, Usill happily briefed his Whitehall friends on the politics of foreign countries. In this case, Usill briefed them not only on Germany but Egypt, a key potential strategic target in any war with the Nazis. He also saw fit to comment on the Nazis' brazen manipulation of politics and sport.

On 4 May 1938, Sir Stephen wrote to Sir Robert Vansittart, the outgoing permanent secretary at the Foreign Office, informing him of Usill's concerns. 'Hitler has made the trainer of the German team into a professor, and it will be a tremendous occasion so that for our prestige it is really important that we should either win or put up a very good fight,' Sir Stephen told Vansittart. 'The German team is already practising and has been doing so for some time. The British team, though it will be selected from the best professionals, has at present the disadvantage that it does not seem likely that it can be got together for practice matches and instruction until shortly before it leaves for Germany.' He suggested sending a 'semi-official' letter to the FA secretary, Stanley Rous, informing him of the UK government's interest in the match.

Rather naively, Sir Stephen suggested to Vansittart that England's internationals should be immediately made available for training with the national squad for the game against Germany. This just happened to be an unrealistic demand. Vansittart's staff, at first, telephoned the FA with their plans, only to be knocked back. The final round of English domestic league fixtures was to be played on 7 May 1938. The destination of the league championship remained in the balance. Under those circumstances, the clubs were not going to release their players.

In the event, a 5-0 victory for Arsenal over Bolton Wanderers and a 1-0 defeat for Wolves at Sunderland meant that the English Football League title headed for Highbury yet again. Pleading phone calls to the FA from the Foreign Office failed to stop England internationals from playing in those games. On the eve of the fixtures, Vansittart formally wrote to the FA with his views on the international against Germany to be played a week later. Tellingly, he referred to the England football team as the British football team. As his letter remained confidential for decades to come, nobody from the SFA, IFA or FAW saw fit to complain.

Vansittart wrote, 'We hear that the German team to play against the British football team in Berlin about a fortnight from now has already been practising for some time, but that the British football team, although it will be selected from the best professionals, can probably not be brought together for practice until very shortly before it leaves for Germany.' He added, 'We hear too, that such importance is being attached to this match in Germany and that it will be treated as a great occasion, so it is really important for our prestige that the British team should put up a really first-class performance. I hope that every possible effort will be made to ensure this.' Rous wrote back on 10 May 1938, 'You may rest assured that every member of the team will do his utmost to uphold the prestige of his country.'

So much for the pretence put up from the British government, of sport having nothing to do with politics. It was pure nonsense. Unless, of course, it considered soft diplomacy to be out of the realms of politics. One issue remained. Given the frenzied preparations for the game, it seemed odd that no protocol had yet been worked out on whether the players ought to offer the Nazi salute during the anthems. It was something not countenanced by British Olympians at the Berlin Games of 1936, but speculation grew that England's footballers might do the opposite and offer the salute, not just for the German anthem *Deutschland Uber Alles* but also the Horst Wessel song. Horst Wessel was a Nazi thug murdered by communists in 1930. His one dubious achievement was to leave behind a song that proved popular among those wrapped up in the cult of Hitler. Thanks to the propaganda skills of Goebbels, Wessel soon became a martyr of the Nazi movement and his song became a Nazi anthem. It rang out as England's footballers made their salute in Berlin. Even on the morning of the game, it remained uncertain that they would do so.

By the time Bert and Stan sat down for their afternoon tea in May 1938, the anti-Semitic signs removed for the Olympics two years earlier were back up. The Nazi newspapers once again poured out their agenda of hate. Even the sports pages promoted notions of Aryan supremacy. Beating their Anglo-Saxon cousins from England at football would serve as another example. Sproston and Matthews reflected on the demands being made of them. It was not simply a matter of going out and winning a football match. Contrary to the view taken at the Olympics, Britain's finest on the sports field were being asked to make the salute. An act of appeasement to be made against the backdrop of rapidly deteriorating European relations.

'Rous and the ambassador reckon Europe's a tinder box,' Matthews told Sproston at their Berlin café. 'So, the powers that be think we might light the spark.' Both men agreed that it was ridiculous to suggest that a bunch of footballers might start a war. Sproston then piped up with his blunt assessment of Hitler. Matthews later recalled that Sproston told him, 'Stan, I'm just a workin' lad. I've not 'ad much of an education and I know nowt 'bout politics and t' like. All I know is football. But t' way I see it, yon 'Itler fella is an evil little twat.'

The Sproston family dispute Matthews's version of events. They do not doubt that the pair went off for a mid-afternoon stroll in Berlin and stopped at a cafe while Hitler went cruising by. But his widow Renee was furious that Matthews chose to credit her husband with the use of crude language. Yes, he thought Hitler was evil. Everyone in Britain did. At least, most did. But Bert was too much of a gentleman to swear. No one doubts the sentiment, however clumsily put by Matthews.

The Stoke City winger recalled his afternoon stroll with the Leeds United defender for David Miller in his biography *Stanley Matthews*, 'I could see that the Germans regarded Hitler as a God. I had not believed such fanaticism was possible,' he told Miller. 'We realised that there was more at stake than merely a football match.'

So, was Henderson bluffing in his comments to Rous? Maybe not. Anxiety, no doubt, drifted through his mind. It is worth noting that in the same month, British ministers feared that they were edging closer to war with Germany than at any time since 1918. Much is understandably made of the Munich agreement and Chamberlain's infamous 'peace for our time' boast in September 1938. But historians also point to the 'May crisis' of 1938 as a key period in the build-up to an inevitable global conflagration. It coincided uneasily with England's footballers touring Europe, beginning in Berlin.

They also set off only weeks after the *Anschluss* – Germany swallowing up Hitler's home country of Austria. The Austrian national team, one of the best in European football between the wars, was disbanded. The England touring squad travelled with Aston Villa FC to Berlin. Villa, were due to play a Greater Germany team – effectively Austria. Not that geopolitics exercised their minds, just beating Germany, Switzerland and France at football mattered.

In between sightseeing around Berlin, the England team went to the Olympiastadion. 'Phew, this has got Wembley knocked into a cocked hat,' commented one of the England players within earshot of British journalists. One of them wondered why the Nazis decided against putting a roof over the stands of such an impressive stadium. The answer was a simple one. 'We do not believe in providing cover, for that would mean discriminating against the poorer fellow, who could not afford to pay the big prices. We think everyone should have the same treatment, and as we cannot cover the whole place then we feel that we should cover none.'

The players also met the German team. Matthews likened them to 'bronzed Greek statues'. Jokingly, he thought that the English players looked 'pretty washed up' by comparison. Rolf, as a Jew, missed out on the programme to turn talented young athletes into human automatons. John MacAdam of the *Sunday Dispatch* noted, 'As we walked round, there in the corner of the sports field was a blond adonis telling a group of other blond adonises (is there such a word?) how to handle a medicine ball! Well, I always thought that all you could do with a medicine ball was chuck it about and have a lot of fun. Apparently, I'm wrong.'

The English visitors, most of them professional sportsmen, left with an insight into how the Nazis treated sport with rigorous scientific application to its development. 'There is not a boy kicking a ball about in the corner whose name does not appear in a filing cabinet in this University of Sport with a note of his potentialities,' concluded MacAdam.

Rolf Friedland's name appeared in a filing cabinet. It just did not belong in any University of Sport. Rolf, to his credit, kept up his levels of fitness along with many other Jewish teenagers in their ad hoc football leagues. Swimming and rowing helped too. He was keener on seeing the England football team in action than monitoring the progress of those singled out by the Nazis as future Olympians and international footballers.

After going their separate ways on sightseeing tours throughout the German capital, the England team gathered for a trip to the theatre. Berlin's Anglo-German society invited them to the Winter Garden Music Hall. Arsenal's trainer, Tom Whittaker, decided he had enough of German songs belted out in a beery atmosphere with a cloud of cigar smoke. The touring party left their seats at the first interval and Whittaker led them to the nearest exit.

They returned to their hotel for a rare taste of five-star food, the type of fare their critics felt they ought not to be eating. All hoped for a good night's sleep ahead of what was rapidly becoming the biggest test of their careers. A football match with political as much as sporting connotations. Young Rolf knew all too well that this was the case. It was reminiscent of the Olympics a couple of years earlier.

The following morning, he slumbered in his bed. 'Wake up!' he told himself before drifting back to sleep. 'Get up! Today's the day!' Rolf lay in his bed as light streamed through the curtains from a dawning sun. It was Saturday morning, 14 May 1938. Rolf planned a new dawn, a fresh life, an escape. He needed to put his ambitious but bizarre plan into action.

Just the mundane matter of heading for the game first. Yes, he was aware of its political importance, knew far better than even any of the Nazi youths working out at the Olympiastadion before the game. But he knew little of how the day might pan out. He was about to witness history.

ENGLAND'S NAZI SALUTE

BERLIN REMAINED in the grip of a heatwave. Spring already gave way to summer. But the bright weather hardly suited the mood of England's finest footballers. On 14 May 1938, they booked their place in British sporting history for all the wrong reasons. Each protested for years afterwards, especially after the war, that they deeply regretted making the Nazi salute in Berlin's Olympiastadion. They insisted it was not their call.

Bert Sproston's daughter-in-law, Janice, recalled how the shame lived with him for the rest of his days. How much he resented the influence of the British establishment. The insistence of the FA and government figures that the players carried out the salute voluntarily angered him. 'The players were all furious.' They did not volunteer, they were ordered to make their controversial gesture.

There was little doubting the appreciation of tens of thousands of German fans. Fanatic served as an apposite description of Hitler's ultra-nationalist devotees. The match was a sell-out. Rolf counted himself lucky to get a ticket to the game. As he walked to the ground amid the bustling crowds in a predictable frenzied atmosphere, Rolf felt his own curious sense of apprehension. It had nothing to do with the outcome of a game of football but everything to do with just how he might engineer a meeting with an England footballer. He kept rehearsing in his mind the English for *autogramm* (autograph).

Anti-Semitic posters displayed amid the Nazi regalia on approaches to the Olympiastadion served as a reminder of his personal reasons for going to the game. Jews, of course, were not welcome in the bars and cafes on the way to the stadium. There was no point in stopping off. No longer welcome in his home city, he wanted to set in motion his plan to leave Nazi Germany. Across the city, his future wife Eva made similar plans, just not as bizarre.

Rolf wore no yellow star, a piece of cloth stigmatising him for his Jewish religious background. It was best to head straight for the ground, no fraternising with the more ebullient fans; he aimed to become more or less invisible, just become immersed in the crowd. Above all, he was determined to avoid any unwarranted attention from the legions of SS and storm troopers monitoring the people. Then once the game was over, he might just be able to engineer an opportunity to escape their attention forever. At the very least, he might be able to meet the English team.

Once inside the vast stadium, Rolf stood almost frozen by emotion. This was an international football match – national patriotism rose to fervent levels absent in other sports. A vast congregation filled the terraces, more of a political and quasi-religious gathering. Not even a football fan's religious experience with pints. Certainly no steins. Not in Hitler's Germany. The creed of Nazism mattered more than any love of the beautiful game.

England's footballers left their hotel at around 3.30pm in time for the 5pm evening kick-off. Time for the temperature to cool down. No chance of the fervent crowd cooling down. The players went up to the dressing room with a curious sense of foreboding. Matters discussed by Sproston and Matthews in a Berlin café took an ominous turn. Whether they would make a Hitler salute in honour of their hosts turned out to be more than just idle gossip. They were going to carry out the infamous act – it was an order.

Aside from any diplomatic problems, it was still an irregular foray back then for England's footballers on foreign soil. For both their legendary winger, Stanley Matthews, and his mate Bert Sproston, it was their first game of international football outside of Great Britain and Ireland. Rather than focusing on football, they spent the build-up aware of the diplomatic briefings, a novelty on tour to put it mildly.

Tactical team-talks were hardly the order of the day. There was no coach either to give advice or to chuck around the proverbial teacups if the match failed to go to plan.

They were about to be offered an alternative role to the one of a professional sportsman. Not a single politician among them, certainly no professional diplomats – that was theoretically Rous's job, his alone. But the second they arrived in a city festooned with Nazi insignia, they were uneasily aware of the political significance of the match. They became unwilling diplomats.

Unfortunately, as the England team gathered that morning for breakfast, the decision about the salute had already been made for them. They would be told or, to be blunt, even ordered to make the Nazi salute as the German anthem was being played.

Charles Wreford-Brown misleadingly briefed English journalists that a decision on the salute would be made at a special meeting held just before kick-off. He described it as an important matter and did not want any misunderstandings. Most sports writers were left with the impression that he had already made his mind up. England's footballers would make the Nazi salute, even with Hitler hundreds of miles away in his Alpine lair. In truth, the decision was made the night before the game, not hours before kick-off.

In the Saturday morning newspapers, Clifford Webb of the *Daily Herald* claimed that Wreford-Brown told him that a Nazi-style salute was almost certain. According to the Press Association correspondent in Berlin, a Nazi or any other salute was customary for visiting football teams. Henry Rose of the *Daily Express* came to a similar conclusion. A Jewish sports journalist, who grew up in Cardiff to immigrant parents, he had tracked with increasing alarm the malevolent interests of the Nazis in sport.

British journalists believed that England's players were on the brink of making history: not a note to be placed in the football record books, but a diplomatic *faux pas*. 'They will create a precedent if they do [make the Nazi salute],' Rose filed from Berlin. 'The gesture would be one of the greatest significance to the crowd of 100,000 who will fill the stadium, but it will be looked upon with mixed feelings by the small English party here.'

As for creating a precedent, the Reuters correspondent in Berlin pointed out an obvious one being put to the FA as they came to a final decision. England's footballers had made a fascist salute for the Italian dictator, Benito Mussolini, in Rome some years earlier. Ivan Sharpe, in Berlin to provide BBC radio commentary, made a similar point. The England team would stand to attention during the playing of 'God Save the King' and then join the home team in making the Nazi salute during the playing of the German anthem. 'The preliminary ceremonial may be similar to that adopted in the match with Italy attended by Signor Mussolini,' he noted.

Players indicated to their friends in the press that they were not happy with the prospect of making a similar mistake again. Sproston and Matthews discussed the matter over their pot of tea in a Berlin café. There was nothing they could do, other than refuse. Hardly a realistic option for a group of working-class lads controlled by their clubs and the FA.

Aside from any political niceties, Rous also thought that the salute could be appropriate because it might put the hostile German crowd in a good temper. England's professional players were quite familiar at domestic level with playing in hostile atmospheres, so it was rather an odd observation from Rous. Most professional footballers relish playing in the finest stadiums, the more febrile the atmosphere, the better. Tens of thousands of German fans began filling the cavernous Olympiastadion hours before kick-off.

England's fans were largely only those with notebooks confined to the press pack. They sat patiently waiting for kick-off under a searing sun in Goebbels's state-of-the-art media facilities installed for the Olympics a couple of years earlier. England's players were gathered in a claustrophobic dressing room located high up in the stands. They sat around waiting, not just to go out to play the match, but also to be told of a formal decision on whether to make the Nazi salute. They already knew the outcome.

Wreford-Brown and Rous had first summoned the captain Eddie Hapgood at the team hotel to inform him of the FA's decision. Before setting off for the Olympiastadion, Hapgood gathered around his team-mates to give them the bad news. Most, including Sproston, already knew. It was still up to the FA officials to tell them all directly. Wreford-Brown waited until the touring party settled in their dressing room.

He then went in to deliver his order. Hapgood's family believed the England captain rather charmingly considered it to be advice rather than an order. Indeed, Rous always insisted the final decision lay with the players. Bert Sproston's daughter-in-law Janice

Sproston insists that they were given no choice. They were angry at being forced to make the Nazi salute.

As they sat in the Olympiastadion, England's players questioned the wisdom of the decision to make the salute. Their pleas were ignored. In some cases, they even did so as late as when they walked out on to the pitch. Eddie Hapgood's daughter Lynne gave an account of how close the players came to rebelling against their FA bosses.

Lynne revealed in her biography *Eddie Hapgood Footballer: From Beyond the Touchline* that her dad even contemplated refusing to lead the team out on to the Olympiastadion pitch. Eddie told his son Tony that he felt the other players would support him, but he could not be sure. He never tested them.

It was Hapgood's duty as England captain to lead them out. The England players laced up their boots, then calmly walked out behind their skipper. They came into the sight of a cheering home crowd alongside their German opponents, led by their captain, Fritz Szepan. Nazi Youth members formed a phalanx across the running track to greet them. The teenage fanatics gave the Nazi salute as the teams walked past them.

Once the teams lined up alongside each other in the middle of the pitch, 'God Save the King' struck up with the German players making the Nazi salute. England's players stood motionless to attention. They wished they had kept doing so. '*Deutschland Uber Alles*' rang out. The English players joined the Germans in making the Nazi salute. They did the same during the playing of the Horst Wessel song. There was no pretence that the English offered a naval salute as they supposedly had done in front of Mussolini some years earlier. They gave the Nazi salute, a gesture in honour of Adolf Hitler.

Even their opposition manager, Sepp Herberger, would look on in puzzlement, if not despair. He had joined the Nazi party in 1933. As a matter of survival under the Nazi regime, he managed to keep his true feelings secret from his fascist overlords. His personal diary notes, certainly those made after the previous game at White Hart Lane, revealed his true disdain for the Nazis. The playing of the Horst Wessel song at Tottenham repulsed him. After the war, US intelligence officers interviewed Herberger as part of their denazification tests. They concluded that the German football coach was not a committed Nazi and he walked free.

After England beat Germany 3-0 in December 1935, Herberger wrote in his diary, 'The national anthems rang out and following ours, again and once more, the *Horst-Wessel-Lied*'.

The England players articulated their discomfort in later years. Hapgood observed after the Second World War, 'I've been V-bombed in Brussels before the Rhine crossing, bombed and "rocketed" in London, I've been in a shipwreck, a train crash, and inches short of a plane accident. But the worst moment of my life, and one I would not willingly go through again, was giving the Nazi salute in Berlin.' He ruefully recalled Nevile Henderson rather patronisingly telling Stanley Rous at the post-match dinner, 'You and your players proved to be good ambassadors after all!'

Hapgood's Arsenal team-mate, Cliff Bastin, confessed to being a little unfazed by the matter. The old ruse of giving the Olympic or naval salute sprang to mind. In his autobiography, *Cliff Bastin Remembers*, written with the help of Brian Glanville, he wrote, 'Personally, I did not feel very strongly about the incident. We had been requested to give the salute by the British Ambassador, in accordance with the insipid policy of appeasement, which was being pursued by the British government at that time. We gave our own salute immediately forwards, and it seemed to me that this palliated any indignity that there might have been in stretching our right arms in the Nazi fashion. If we had been requested to give the Nazi sign alone, then I would have been angry. Certainly, the German crowd appreciated our action. They cheered us to the echo.'

Stanley Matthews gave his account of events in a series of autobiographies. In 1948, he wrote *Feet First,* a book dedicated more to making his excuses over a controversial move from Stoke City to Blackpool. Recalling the Nazi salute in Berlin a decade earlier, he commented, 'Even to this day I still feel shame whenever I sit by the fire and glance through my scrap book and gaze on that infamous picture of an England football team lining up like a bunch of Nazi robots giving the dreaded salute.'

Just before he died in the year 2000, Sir Stanley insisted in *The Way it Was* that he wanted to put the record straight. If anything, the controversy over England's Nazi salute intensified during the decades after the war. Matthews described bedlam in the dressing room once Wreford-Brown had told them to give the Nazi salute. He wrote, 'All the players were livid and totally opposed to this, myself included. Everyone was shouting at once. Eddie Hapgood, normally a respectful and devoted captain, wagged his finger at the official and told him what he could do with the Nazi salute, which involved putting it where the sun doesn't shine.'

According to Matthews, Sir Nevile Henderson had not only advised them to give the Nazi salute but had delivered a 'direct order' to do so; one endorsed by Rous. Again, this account directly contradicts Rous's version of events. It is also slightly at odds with Hapgood's version. Beyond Matthews and Hapgood, many of the England players felt they had been badly let down and hung out to dry. Matthews wrote, 'I sat there crestfallen thinking what on earth my family and the people back home would think if they saw me and the rest of the England team paying lip service, so to speak, to the Nazi regime and its leaders.'

Matthews believed the team had little choice, given the pressure being applied by Henderson on behalf of the British government. He said the players were told by the hapless Wreford-Brown that the political situation between Great Britain and Germany was so volatile it only needed a 'spark to set Europe alight'. Matthews concluded, 'Faced with the knowledge of the direst consequences, we felt we had little choice in the matter and reluctantly agreed to the request.'

The infamous photograph of the England team making the Nazi salute still pops up in any discussions of sport and politics. Stanley Matthews described its publication in the national newspapers as ensuring the eternal shame of every player. As far as one of England's greatest ever footballers was concerned, they all felt they had let their country down.

Matthews recalled in his 1960 autobiography *The Stanley Matthews Story*, 'As I glanced at the tense England players all talking and shouting at the same time, my thoughts flew back home to Stoke and Hanley. What would my family and townsfolk say if they saw a photograph of me giving the Nazi salute? My mind went numb. I glanced round the room again and a deep sense of fear entered my heart. I thought this was the end of the match – before it had begun.'

Bert Sproston made no public comment on being told to make the Nazi salute, complying with the order. His family insisted it was a source of shame. He regretted making the gesture for the rest of his life. Giving in to Henderson and Rous was a grave mistake.

He shared the views of his friend Stanley Matthews. Their minds went numb.

Back home, England's salute prompted condemnation. It was by no means universal. As for those responsible, the FA and the British government made concerted efforts in later years to lay all the blame on the players. At the time, they praised them. Once war broke out, they blamed them. Few believed the FA and ministers, those wedded to the policy of appeasement. Clear and considerable pressure appeared to be applied on the players by diplomats, government ministers and FA committee men.

Such an assessment was something the Foreign Office clearly did not share. It sent congratulatory missives to the Football Association. For the FA committee members to make such an important and sensitive diplomatic decision that late seems distinctly odd. For there to be claims of no British government input into the decision to make the Nazi salute, given the Foreign Office's almost panic-stricken missive to the FA only a few days earlier, was also curious. Making the salute during the German anthem was bad enough. Doing the same during a song glorifying one of Hitler's street-fighting thugs only compounded the matter.

Nothing surprised Rolf. He looked on impassively as Nazi pre-match rituals descended into pseudo-religious fervour. It was all too predictable, all too familiar. England's footballers gave Hitler and his henchmen their propaganda victory. Winning the football match? Only one winner for Rolf. It was England.

Out of the corner of their eyes as they made the Nazi salute, they spotted the Union flag. It was flown in those days for England games rather than the cross of St George. They fixed upon the flag, hoping it would draw inspiration. The trick worked.

Sporting etiquette apparently satisfied, all protocols fulfilled, England went off on a spring stroll around the park. Berlin's Olympiastadion, admittedly thanks to a few upgrades, remains as one of sport's most impressive stadiums to this day. England's footballers enjoyed its environs in 1938. Their performance seemed worthy of the masters of the world game.

As much as the match itself served up some great entertainment, it was almost an irrelevance for historians. Some rather lazily describe the English footballers' Nazi salute as an act of 'virtue signalling' – an odd politically unsophisticated comment. It does not work as a criticism in the 21st century, let alone in an era long before the term found its way into an English dictionary. Neither Ralph nor the England team deemed it virtuous. Nor a signal for Nazi approval. Quite the opposite.

It was a misguided diplomatic act carried out by a group of footballers under duress. One ordered by their bosses, the FA, and a UK government intent on the pursuit of appeasement. However, at the time, the sporting encounter mattered the most to fans. England's faltering football team was taking on an ambitious, but limited, Germany team. Ralph stood on the terraces in unison with the sparse scattering of England supporters.

The ugliness of the pre-match rituals over, they embraced the beautiful game. Germany were thrashed 6-3 yet players and fans were magnanimous in defeat. German fans, those allowed to offer an opinion, emerged feeling bizarrely quite comfortable with how events unfolded. *Fußball Woche,* the in-house journal of the DFB, even went as far as hailing England as world champions.

Perhaps any anger at being forced to make this infamous gesture emboldened the English players during the game itself. England gave what even German football fans declared as a masterclass.

They were doubly satisfied by events in the Olympiastadion – a distinctly odd state of mind for a bunch of football fans.

Henry Rose expressed his delight in the *Daily Express* at the comfortable victory. Then again, a correspondent more than familiar with Nazi abuse of sport was less than enamoured with England's behaviour before kick-off. England's salute left this Jewish journalist feeling cold. In securing the win on the football pitch, English prestige in sport had rocketed 'sky-high.' Germany took a reminder from the masters of football that its footballers were merely pupils of the game. But the lesson came at a price.

Rose's most telling observation was not, of course, of the game itself. Rose lamented, 'My lasting impression is not of the play of either side, not of the crowd in this magnificent concrete arena that makes you catch your breath when you first see it, not of the orderliness and perfection of organisation that sees this huge army of 110,000 marshalled in and out like clockwork. No. My lasting impression is of 11 professional English footballers lined up in the centre of the field giving the Nazi salute as the band strikes up *'Deutschland Uber Alles'* and the Horst Wessel [song].'

The *Daily Express* offered an observation that might even unsettle his own fascist-supporting proprietor. Lord Beaverbrook embraced Nazi hospitality at the 1936 Berlin Olympics. It was just the latest act of appeasement, a policy eagerly endorsed by Beaverbrook's *Daily Express*. Rose counselled that the England players were not happy about it. This legendary figure of British sports writing made it clear that the players told him they were unhappy with being told to make the salute. One anonymous player spoke of his fear that his father would see the photograph in the newspaper. He would not be pleased. There appeared a sense of relief among them as they lowered their arms.

Intriguingly, Rose also speculated that there was no unanimity about the decision to make the salute among the FA committee in charge of the touring party. Theoretically, they were in a position to ignore the advice of the British ambassador to Berlin. In reality, they were left with little choice.

Matthews later revealed that he was comforted by the sight of a Union flag waved by a gaggle of English fans, most likely diplomats based at the Berlin embassy. Travel from Britain to Nazi Germany was discouraged. In any case, fans did not go to international games in large numbers in those days. It was simply unaffordable. Rolf knew that a plan to use meagre savings to go to a game in England was a little bold, perhaps foolish.

Once the English players had delivered the infamous salute and won the match convincingly, the British ambassador, Sir Nevile Henderson, expressed delight. Sir Nevile deemed not only England's performance in winning 6-3, but also the pre-match Nazi salute with its warm reception from the German crowd, a success. To sum up, he boasted that the match 'undoubtedly revived in Germany, British sporting prestige'.

History would record it as one of the most infamous moments in British sport, yet the senior British diplomat to the Nazi regime was fulsome in his praise. In fairness, he had other matters to consider. In the diplomatic crisis of May 1938, it is tempting to argue that the politeness of England's footballers helped him. More likely, it made no difference. The match led to the Foreign Office taking the unprecedented step of writing to the FA to thank the organisation for its role in helping to cement Anglo-German relations.

The FA boss, Stanley Rous, felt he was in no position in later years to ignore the angry response from critics. Rous made his excuses, citing the dubious advice given by Sir Nevile Henderson. For good measure, he blamed the players as willing participants. Rous claimed rather unconvincingly, 'All agreed that they had no objection, and no doubt saw it as a bit of fun rather than of any political significance.' Most of the players begged to differ.

One of the curiosities in what Rous dismissed as a bit of fun just happened to be the tale of Stan Cullis. According to football folklore, the Wolves centre-half and the club's future legendary manager, refused to make the salute on the day of the game. He allegedly offered the immortal words, 'Count me out!' If true, he was the one man who apparently refused to give in to pressure and go along with the plan. Cullis was allegedly dropped from the side to play Germany just before kick-off. It is a good story. It also appears to be a myth.

England's team to play Germany was named by the selectors on Friday, 29 April 1938. Cullis was not one of the 11 players named on the England team sheet. Critics felt he had played poorly in the 1-0 defeat to Scotland at Wembley earlier in the month. Cullis complained of an injury. He went on tour as a travelling reserve with the promise of a game against Switzerland or France. A bout of sea sickness on the short ferry trip across the English Channel hardly helped him. Quite whether he objected to England's players making the Nazi salute before even leaving for Germany is something of a moot point. Contrary to football folklore, he was certainly not dropped on the day of the game. Cullis watched from the stands as his colleagues made the Nazi salute.

The England captain, Hapgood, admitted that he felt 'a fool *heiling* Hitler' but the curious act of diplomacy on behalf of the FA worked for him because it made his side more determined to go out and beat the Germans. Once the match kicked off, only the weather conditions bothered him. He said in his pre-match comments, 'We have never yet played in such heat and all our players suffered under it. In cool weather we would have done still better. The Germans fought well, but we who saw the Germans in 1935 in London believe that the Germans were stronger three years ago, especially in defence.'

Matthews described it as the finest England performance he had ever been involved with. In England's 6-3 victory the goalscorers were Cliff Bastin (Arsenal), Jackie Robinson (Sheffield Wednesday), Frank Broome (Aston Villa), Stanley Matthews (Stoke City) and Len Goulden (West Ham United). Robinson scored twice on his international debut. The only disappointment happened to be conceding three goals against the run of play. Most observers felt that Vic Woodley, the England goalkeeper, had little to do. But he still, to his frustration, let in three goals.

Bastin opened the scoring after 15 minutes with a goal described as a cracker by his Arsenal team-mate, Hapgood. Unfortunately, the English defenders were as overly generous to their German opponents during the game as before it. Germany equalised less than five minutes later. From a corner three German players were left unmarked, and Rudi Gellesch took the simple opportunity to score. England quickly restored their lead. Bastin crossed for Robinson, who flashed the ball into the corner of the net. Villa's centre-forward Frank Broome tormented the German defence for the entire game (and carried on in the next day's match for his club against a Greater Germany XI). He raced past a couple of dozing defenders to make it 3-1 after just half an hour played.

Robinson then set up Matthews's goal to make it 4-1 just before half-time. 'I received a beauty of a pass from Robinson,'

Matthews recalled. 'My pace was enough to take me past two German defenders and just as I cut into the penalty area I let fly.' Much to his frustration, there was still time for Germany to nick a goal from Josef Gauchel before the players walked off for a break. Matthews remembered his team going back to the dressing room behaving as a bunch of high-spirited young lads heading for their local pub on a night out.

England went back into a three-goal lead only four minutes after the interval. This time Matthews returned the compliment to Robinson, who beat the German goalkeeper Hans Jakob from 20 yards out. Germany just about stayed in the game thanks to a misunderstanding between Bert Sproston and Woodley, which allowed Johann Pesser to score. Despite his error, Sproston won praise for his performance. Henry Rose wrote that Sproston and the England captain, Eddie Hapgood, were brilliant. Charles Buchan shared this opinion. He also boasted that England were 'supreme' in the football world.

The Press Association correspondent, Hubert Grant, was less sure. He criticised Hapgood for not organising the defence properly. He also noted, 'Sproston's tackling was delightfully neat, and he made some great recoveries which several times aroused applause, though actually he has played better.'

The best of the game's nine goals was the last. Len Goulden brought down a cross from Matthews with five minutes left and half-volleyed the ball into the net. *The Times* correspondent contended that the strike drew gasps of admiration from the crowd. Henry Rose of the *Daily Express* simply described it as a goal that all footballers dream about, a fitting finale to the game.

Such was the confidence of the Nazis, they had supposedly commissioned a special eagle trophy to be presented to the winning

German team, a plan that was well and truly scuppered. Instead of presenting the trophy to the winning captain, Eddie Hapgood, Nazi officials spirited it away. There was to be no souvenir of victory, just the photograph of England's winning team making the Nazi salute before the game kicked off.

Nazi newspapers declared, 'The English are still the perfect artists.' In the days following the game, *Fußball Magazin* reserved the greatest praise for England's wingers. 'One hasn't seen wingers in Germany of the calibre of Matthews and Bastin for years, not the kind of flank attack they were capable of delivering relentlessly,' it declared. 'Matthews even surpassed Bastin with his unbelievable speed and drive for goal. Technically Bastin, too, was supreme, but Matthews excelled.'

Offering up the pretence of promoting international sporting friendship, the Nazis were the perfect con artists. Naturally enough the Nazi Party's newspaper, *Völkischer Beobachter*, published a photograph of England's footballers with their salute and celebrated this so-called act of courtesy. 'The action of the Englishmen in raising their right arms in greeting during the playing of the German national anthems and in taking leave of the game was particularly well received,' it commented. 'In itself probably only a gesture of politeness; but when one knows the disinclination of English footballers for every kind of formality, this proof of esteem of comradely feeling should be particularly emphasised.'

The *Daily Herald* triumphantly commented, 'This was the football fairy story come true – an England eleven on the Continent playing like a set of soccer professors in an exhibition game and looking good enough to toy with any team in the world.' The England players' ability to overcome a mini-heatwave in Berlin and travel weariness earned them praise as much as the quality of their football. John Thompson of the *Daily Mirror* rather pompously declared, 'The win shows that, in some respects, the masters still hold their mastery, that foreign pupils of our great game have still to become over-precocious in their lessons.' Charles Buchan in the *News Chronicle* gave his seal of approval. To him, England demonstrated their superiority from the start in all phases of the game.

Ivan Sharpe, a man in awe of the state-of-the-art broadcast facilities the Nazis offered for the BBC, gloried in the English victory. To him, England's Nazi salute served as just a matter of politeness to the hosts. Sharpe said the English players stunned a six-figure crowd filling a cavernous stadium into silence. The players had struck a resounding blow for British sporting prestige and did so on the eve of the World Cup in Paris. It was somehow a tournament the England football team need not bother to play in; Sharpe was by no means alone in holding such an opinion.

The message sent home was a simple one. England maintained British prestige as masters of world football. Better still, Germans declared them world champions. It was the main focus of the coverage in Fleet Street newspapers, rather than the dubious behaviour with the Nazi salute before the game. *Fussball Woche*, the DFB official magazine, added in its coverage, 'The English remain unparalleled champions – enchanting perfect play. They are world champions of football after all, these English.'

Stanley Rous of the FA purred, 'It was a splendid game. We are glad we won by such a good margin. The boys are delighted with the result. They particularly admired the sportsmanship of the crowd. You can see we greatly appreciated the attitude of everyone – referee, officials, opposing players and the crowd.' No doubt his hosts appreciated the England players making the salute. Curiously, they also potted all the takings from the game. Quite bizarrely, the FA was so anxious to please its hosts, it agreed to the Nazi-controlled DFB keeping all the gate money. Not only did the FA grant the Nazis a propaganda victory, but they also effectively paid for the privilege.

Rous saw no problem in them taking the money and his players making such a dubious diplomatic gesture. Much to his delight, agreement was reached to play another international between the two countries in England, sometime in 1940. Instead, the Battle of Britain took place, the fabled few of the RAF bravely thwarting the Luftwaffe and scuppering Hitler's plans for a military invasion of England. Ironically, a few of the England footballers lining up in May 1938, including Stanley Matthews, signed up for the RAF at the outbreak of the Second World War. Bert Sproston enlisted in the army.

After 90 minutes of intense football in gruelling conditions, he was exhausted. He had had enough of bumping into Germans with a love of football. But there was to be one more. Rolf's goal differed markedly from any of the other 100,000 or so inside the stadium. England's right-back unwittingly allowed him, metaphorically, to score. Forget England's errant pre-match diplomacy. In one isolated case, defence was about to be turned into attack. Little did Sproston know but he was ultimately about to recruit another member of the British Army, a young German football fan. Rolf Friedland's novel escape plan was about to work.

THE AUTOGRAPH HUNTER

ROLF GINGERLY walked down the Olympiastadion stairwells as he made his way out of the vast arena. He took care not to be swept away by the huge crowd. Judging by the behaviour of the other fans, he felt there was a danger of being sent tumbling down the steps. An added peril was being wrapped up in a weird sense of hysteria. Germany lost but the home crowd seemed to care little. It was as if the Nazis had drugged the crowd.

England impressed Rolf. They were not only the inventors but the true masters of the global game. England's footballers had just thrashed the German fans' football idols. Did it matter? Did sporting pride count? Not quite. More importantly to a crowd in thrall to the Nazis, England had paid tribute to Hitler by offering a salute. Excitable and loyal German fans concluded that this bunch of true English gentlemen signalled England's intent to be friends of the Nazis. The English players thought no such thing.

The propaganda trick worked better than any free-kick routine from off the training pitch. Goebbels was no sporting tactical genius but sadly, he was a political one. Sport only mattered as a political vehicle to be abused. Once the political choreography was over, even the most fanatical Nazis oddly shared Rolf's favourable view of the England football team's sporting merits. Although

Germany were defeated, the sight of the English footballers lining up to make the salute meant it was honours even for the Nazis – a score draw in football parlance.

Even so, England's players enthusiastically celebrated their sporting triumph. Best to forget the enforced political antics. Bert Sproston sat in the dressing room draped in a towel, merely satisfied with the result. He was too exhausted to join his team-mates in celebration. Then came a knock on the door and Stanley Rous walked in with the ambassador to Berlin, Sir Nevile Henderson, to offer his congratulations. The British establishment considered the Nazi salute to be a job well done, not just the playing performance but the infamous salute.

Bert Sproston still felt some unease after hearing the British ambassador congratulating the England team in their dressing room. What for? Winning the match? Fair enough. Embarrassing themselves by making the Nazi salute, paying tribute to the evil little man, Hitler? No.

Bert stood up to leave and looked down at his peg. He left his boots, matchday shorts and socks for the kitman and trainer, Arsenal's Tom Whittaker. He picked up his precious England shirt with the three lions on the crest for safe keeping. The game left him in a state of delirium. A generous warm bath and a few celebratory chilled Prussian beers in the dressing room had failed to fully revive him. If anything, he felt worse. Such had been Bert's commitment during the match in a blistering hot sun, he left the ground dehydrated and exhaustion had set in.

Hundreds of fans waited outside for the England team, oddly mostly German fans being friendly towards their esteemed visitors. Sport can bring people together in the spirit of respect, even friendship. It is not just, as Orwell claimed, war minus the bullets. Goebbels, the Nazi propaganda minister, no doubt agreed with Orwell. Just one obvious caveat: he called for total war.

On the streets outside, Rolf briefly became distracted by the post-match verdict delivered in the Berlin newspapers, having appeared on the streets at lightning speed. A quick glance confirmed the worst. England's Hitler salute appeared to be of more importance than a humiliating 6-3 defeat. Rolf paused in despair. He had more important matters to attend to than reading the nonsense in Nazi propaganda newssheets.

Among the hubbub, the German teenager discovered a source of salvation although the person he spotted did not immediately look like one. An England defender cutting a bedraggled figure after a tough afternoon in the cauldron of the Olympiastadion packed with more than 100,000 hostile fans. Little did this extremely tired footballer know he was about to save a refugee from oppression. Making the Nazi salute? To be condemned forever? The chance for redemption was about to be grasped by a young man from Sandbach in Cheshire.

Only at that moment, Bert was too mentally and physically frazzled to notice. No belated endorphin rush from his exertions during the game, simply a desire to leave the Nazi cathedral of sport. His professionalism kicked in as he was surrounded by admirers, oddly German well-wishers.

One mental reminder for Rolf as he joined the crowd of fans. Just avoid any unwarranted attention from the hundreds of jackbooted Nazi storm troopers, Gestapo and police. Happily, consumed by the throng of football fans, they were oblivious to any interaction between Rolf and Bert. Just another fan delaying the England team's departure from the stadium.

There was no chance of the team returning to their hotel on time. No matter that on the quiet an escape plan was being hatched. The jackboots' preening bosses were blissfully unaware. So too, the British ambassador and his staff. At least in theory until an unusual letter from the FA dropped through the embassy letter box some weeks later. All they witnessed in the post-match excitement was a spot of autograph hunting from kids and teenagers. All perfectly innocent.

Why would any of them want to escape their native land? Only if it had become a hostile land. So much so that an England football scarf would have been preferable for Rolf than a stigmatising yellow star. He wore neither.

For his mission, any player would do. He nervously approached them. Alan Freeman told me that his dad admitted in later life that he had doubts and almost decided to abandon his plan. Ralph convinced himself that he was unable to leave without trying. Surely, someone might help? To unashamedly use a football cliché with regards to what was about to happen, Rolf Friedland managed to hit the back of the net.

Nobody bothered to approach Bert Sproston apart from Rolf and it took Bert by surprise. At the time, the exhausted England player just wanted to board the coach and head for the hotel. Aches and pains overcame him, it would be difficult even to board the steps of the coach. But as a dedicated professional footballer there was no way he was going to shun the fans.

Rolf looked around, trying to avoid untoward attention from police and security. He was just another friendly fan, a German kid besotted with football, nothing to worry Nazi guards. Rolf then approached Bert. 'Sir, autograph! Can I have your autograph please?' All very routine. Bert scribbled down his signature for Rolf.

As Bert handed back his autographed paper, Rolf persisted in making the most of his prize encounter. 'Sir, sir, please read,' Rolf pleaded. 'Sorry, my English, not very good. Er, Nazis stopped school. Expelled is the word, yah?' The young German football fan handed over his name and sparse details.

His broken English was fine, understandable enough for someone with a south Cheshire accent. Bert briefly perused the note. At the heart of Rolf's plan was an exhibition football match. England were due to play a Rest of Europe side at Highbury later in the year as part of the FA's 75th anniversary celebrations. Bert Sproston, by then an England regular, was expected to play. Could he get Rolf a ticket for the game?

Bert looked at him, a little dazed and confused. The physical travails of the game he had just played hardly helped. Rolf persisted in broken English. 'I need to get out of Germany,' he begged. Rolf told him that he needed permission to leave Germany, to enter England. Could the England footballer arrange it? He needed not only a ticket for the match but also a visa. Sproston did not know at the time whether he would be selected for the England game against the Rest of Europe at Highbury. It was still five months off.

Bert was unable to fathom the reasons at the time himself but he offered to help the young German football fan. The encounter had taken him by surprise. Notes dutifully placed in his pocket, Bert boarded the coach. Finally, he was able to rest.

Perhaps relief for Rolf. But his encounter with the England full-back surprisingly made him feel uneasy. Would Mr Sproston deliver on his promise? It was far from certain. What promise? Just a polite few words to see off a pest of a fan. Rolf left the stadium feeling more than a tad nervous. As a German football fan wanting the country's national team to lose, he was a rarity. He was pleased, even relieved, that England had won. The Nazis had lost. As for his escape plans, they were left in the lap of the football gods.

Rolf (latterly Ralph) passed away some years ago, so his son Alan Freeman told me of his father's exploits after the game and the key role of the England defender. Alan reflected, 'As my father is no longer alive, I have to rely on my memory, on what I remember he told me about how he escaped from Berlin.' The game itself between Germany and England remained something of a blur. Alan said, 'Knowing my father, his mind would have been preoccupied with extracting himself out of Germany to save his life, rather than on the game. Would his plan to approach an England player work?'

Alan never doubted that Sproston saved his father's life. Indeed, he in turn was grateful to Bert Sproston for his own life. It was all down to his intervention not only immediately after the game in Berlin but the following weeks. Sproston and Matthews might well have dismissed the FA boss, Stanley Rous, as a pompous old ref as they sat in a Berlin café. But winning over Rous would be vital in any attempt to bring Rolf to England.

For Bert, purloining a ticket for a football match might not be a problem. As for sponsoring a visa for entry to Britain, it was a different matter. Bert was not really sure of where to start. Bert joked that a passport was needed for a journey between Cheshire and Staffordshire. Obtaining a visa for a complete stranger to enter England from Nazi Germany posed a near impossible challenge.

At worst, it meant dealing with the likes of ambassador Henderson. At best, it meant dealing with the FA and Rous, not much of an improvement. But Sproston knew he needed Rous's assistance, not that he was going to raise the matter immediately at their Berlin hotel.

Alan Freeman's wife, Sue Surkes, wrote of her father-in-law's encounter with the England team on that fateful day in Berlin for the *Times of Israel*. Sue made her comments on 26 July 2022 as Spurs were due to play a pre-season friendly against AS Roma in Haifa. Much attention focused on the reunion of the Spurs players with their old manager, Jose Mourinho, but she, quite understandably, wanted to inform her readers of a more heart-warming tale than any involving personal animosity in a pre-season clash of modern UEFA Champions League clubs.

She described the unlikely meeting between a desperate young Jewish fan and an England footballer. Additionally, she noted that Sproston had been no fan of the Nazis. In truth, neither were the rest of the England team. She wrote in the *Times of Israel*, 'Thanks to Sproston's singular act of humanity, though, Ralph [Rolf] was saved.'

Did Rolf Friedland act alone? His son Alan is not sure. Rolf's request in broken English went beyond just asking a random international footballer for a match ticket. It was much more detailed. German fans would be allowed to go to Britain for the game in question, given that the DFB agreed to release players for FIFA's Rest of Europe team. Rolf was hardly going to enrol into the Nazis' Strength through Joy programme or be accepted for enrolment. Therefore, he needed an alternative method of securing a UK visa under newly introduced British regulations. It is likely that this headstrong and resourceful teenager did receive help from Berlin's Jewish community.

Francis R. Nicosia and David Scrase highlight remarkable community efforts in their work, *Jewish Life in Nazi Germany*. Ever since the 19th century in imperial Germany, religious groups were subject to taxation. Forget the habit of sending around the collection plate or basket at Catholic mass in other countries, just pay your taxes. Worshippers at synagogues were no exception. Nicosia and Scrase maintained that taxes and voluntary contributions enabled the Jewish community to build up a welfare network. It may have been of limited help. But it was still useful once the Nazis came to power. They acknowledge troubling aspects, not least a degree of co-operation with the Nazi authorities.

Up until spring 1938, one such welfare organisation happened to be the *Reichsvertretung der Deutschen Juden* [Reich representation of German Jews], an organisation controversially still co-operating with the Nazis. But conversely, it still tried to cope with the economic, political and personal persecution of Jews. This included assistance with emigration. Critics identified such work as too uncomfortably close to *Judenrein*, cleansing Germany of Jews.

Another network assisted Germany's Jewish population since 1901. *Hilfsverein der Deutschen Juden* focused in its early years on education and social welfare. After the Great War it began to help Jews emigrate abroad. Once the Nazis came to power, this involved helping Jews to emigrate to destinations other than Palestine. Once the Nuremberg Laws were passed in 1935, it intensified its work, offering English lessons for those wanting to go to Britain, the United States or Canada.

Rolf's family had already emigrated from Germany, leaving him alone to fend for himself. Quite whether the *Reichsvertretung*, *Hilfsverein der Deutschen Juden* or other German Jewish self-help groups in Berlin assisted him is a matter of conjecture. But he certainly needed someone with a strong command of English to draw up a detailed note of Rolf's visa requirements. Did any of his friends know their precious notes were to be given to an England footballer? If so, no doubt they thought the German teenager was mad. Nevertheless, England's Bert Sproston left Berlin with a German fan's request for a ticket for an England game later in the year, plus details to support an application.

Bert had looked forward to the post-match banquet in Berlin, a regular party for players and officials alike for international events, although he arrived back at the team hotel, feeling unwell. The last thing he needed was the fine food on offer at a five-star hotel. He missed the celebrations, going straight to bed. The Leeds United manager, Billy Hampson, travelled with the England team to Berlin and helped Sproston up to his room. The player had much to reflect on before drifting off to sleep, not just the match but his chance encounter with the anxious German fan.

OFF TO WHITE HART LANE

BERT LEFT Berlin confused but happy. Just why did he agree to help the random German fan outside Berlin's Olympiastadion? As a fine young Englishman, honour mattered. He gave his word that he would help. Quite how was another matter. But he resolved to answer a heartfelt plea of desperation. It was important, especially as he was unable to answer to his personal satisfaction another question: just why did he make the Nazi salute along with his mates?

On the following morning, there was a knock on the door. No chance of a Sunday lie-in. From outside in the corridor his visitor expressed a cry of concern. 'You alright Bert?' 'Yes,' he replied before climbing out of bed and opening the door. His club manager, Billy Hampson, stood outside. Bert told his boss that he was feeling much better and had enjoyed a good night's sleep. He might have a warm, soothing bath, then join everyone for breakfast. Hampson expressed his relief. There was genuine concern on his part. He was not just being a typical mercenary, soulless football manager. Sproston had ended up on the point of collapse after playing in gruelling heat. His health was a worry. And there was another concern.

One other Football League manager just happened to be prowling the hotel corridors. Hampson wanted to keep his young star out of the way of the Aston Villa boss Jimmy Hogan. Rumours abounded that Leeds United might be willing to sell Sproston and Hogan could be interested. Hampson wanted to keep Sproston. His board thought otherwise.

Villa were due to play a Greater Germany team later that day. It was mostly the old Austrian national team – the *Wunderteam* of European football at one time. Hogan was assistant to Austria's legendary manager, Hugo Meisl. Hogan even joked that he once helped to train most of the opposition team.

One thing mystified hotel staff. He was as big a football star in central Europe as some players, certainly bigger than members of his team but his command of German just happened to be surprisingly poor. At a training session with young kids, he needed an interpreter. As for English, he was blunt and undiplomatic, and he always insisted to the Germans or Austrians that he was Irish. Hogan was the proud son of Irish immigrants.

The Villa players watched England play the previous day. One of them, Frank Broome, played for England. He was to play again, this time for his club. Once again, more than 100,000 spectators flocked to Berlin's Olympiastadion.

On the previous day, the atmosphere for Germany versus England once the match went ahead was mute. It was almost polite – Sproston and Matthews winning applause on the right wing. It was not just from fans they charmed in a Berlin café the day before the game.

Villa won a much more febrile match against Greater Germany 2-1. The result of the match mattered little. Bert and his team-mates might be forgiven for a little chuckle once more controversy ensued. Unlike the England team, Villa refused to offer a Nazi salute. They were supposed to do so at the end of the game but many of the players stormed off instead. Villa's captain, Jimmy Allen, stood in the middle of the pitch, trying to, and failing to call them back. As a chorus of boos rang around the stadium, the band trying to drown them out, Allen gave up. He walked off, no Nazi salute to be made.

Hogan revealed that the FA had asked his players to make the Nazi salute before leaving the field. Indeed, club officials assured the FA that they would do so. The players' decision to refuse, Hogan reasoned, was entirely 'spontaneous' and due to the bad-tempered nature of the game. His players made no such excuses, not least Allen. 'Our boys resented the fact that before the England–Germany game, when the English players stood to attention during the playing of our national anthem, the Germans gave the Nazi salute,' Villa's captain told reporters after the game. He also made it clear that the entire team was unhappy at going along with the diplomatic protocol of offering a Nazi salute. It was unacceptable to them.

FA officials took the opposite view. Aston Villa players' refusal to give a salute after the game somehow embarrassed them. They were of the belief that the offering of the salute by the England football team served as an act of sporting politeness, a job well done. All their diplomatic work had been destroyed by the stubborn refusal of the Villa players to repeat the gesture after their match with the so-called Greater Germany team.

Publicly, Villa's directors passed off the refusal to stay behind after the game to offer the salute as a 'misunderstanding'. They put out a statement reading, 'After a match in Germany, it is customary to give the Nazi salute. As soon as the final whistle went, our players carried on as they usually do and the failure to give the salute was purely a misunderstanding.' Hogan, at first only anxious to talk about football and rows over tactics, eventually went along with his bosses and sold this curious version of events.

The England and Villa players went their separate ways. Bert Sproston and his team-mates set off for Zurich for a match against Switzerland. The Villa team remained in Germany for more tour matches. They agreed to make the salute. The presence of Nazi storm troopers and the SS focused their minds. There was zero point in doing otherwise, however difficult. After all, they were just a bunch of footballers.

Any illusions of grandeur on the part of England's footballers lasted just one week. They lost 2-1 to Switzerland on Saturday, 21 May 1938. Stan Cullis was still unable to command a place in the England side. Goalkeeper Vic Woodley was hailed as man of the match. 'Swiss roll over England at soccer' was just one unimpressed Sunday newspaper headline. Ivan Sharpe described the English defeat as a nasty surprise. The Swiss hailed a 'miracle'. The captain, Severino Minelli, rather graciously commented, 'We had a lucky day. We were on our game and the English players were off theirs.'

Once again, Sproston's place in the England side was in doubt. To compound matters, he gave away the penalty that allowed Switzerland to score the winning goal. *Reynolds News* told its readers, 'In the 73rd minute Lauro Amadò crossed the ball into the centre, where Sproston, standing in the penalty area, allowed the ball to touch his hands. Dr [Peco] Bauwens did not to fail to see this infringement, which appeared unintentional, and he once again pointed without hesitation to the spot.'

Reynolds News felt that the German referee missed earlier infringements from Switzerland. Bauwens, whose Jewish wife later died from suicide at the outbreak of war, courted controversy throughout his career. After West Germany won the 1954 World

Cup, Bauwens, who had become boss of the DFB, was admonished by the country's president for making a speech replete with Nazi terminology and backing the *führer* principle.

Theodor Heuss admonished the man he called 'the good Bauwens' and informed him along with other like-minded people that 'a good kicking does not make good politics'. Refereeing a football match was easier than dabbling in domestic or global politics.

André 'Trello' Abegglen sent the Swiss crowd into a frenzy as he scored the winning goal from the penalty spot. Charles Wreford-Brown commented after the game, 'Switzerland played exceedingly and surprisingly well. They are one of the best teams we have met in the last few years.' Despairing Fleet Street correspondents agreed with the Swiss captain's assessment and England's footballers had been poor.

Fleet Street writers criticised the England players' attitude during their European tour. Yes, the game in Berlin was taken seriously. But the likes of Sproston and Matthews ought not to go out sightseeing in the German capital. They were professional sportsmen, not tourists. Henry Rose of the *Daily Express* was annoyed enough by the sight of them making the Nazi salute before the Germany game, blaming the FA, but he held back from calling out the players given their victory. Not so, a week later.

After the defeat to Switzerland, criticism flowed that the England team was on holiday. As professional footballers, they were not taking their duties seriously. 'The players had a grand time,' Rose ranted. 'Make no mistake about it. The experience of seeing foreign countries, the change of scenery and all that goes with it, is the one thing they will never forget. But business never did mix with pleasure. No one can convince me that staying in the most expensive hotels and eating rich food, to which they are not accustomed, is the right preamble to a big football match.'

On a more positive note, Rose mentioned that the Swiss simply had a job to do. There were no salutes, no bands and no anthems, just a football match. And, unlike the Germans, the Swiss did it well.

It was agreed before the players set out on tour that everyone would be given a game. Consequently, Stan Cullis returned to the England side for the game against France at the Stade Colombes in Paris on 26 May 1938. Sproston kept his place. It had been expected that Arthur Bateman of Brentford would play instead but the selectors left him out. Bateman never won an England cap.

England won 4-2 and after the travails of Berlin, followed by defeat in Zurich for England, the game in Paris passed off in a friendly way, with opposing players sharing a welcome beer in the dressing rooms afterwards. There was no controversy for them to discuss.

A record crowd in France, estimated at almost 70,000, turned out to watch the faltering English masters. It was a number which was not beaten during the course of the 1938 World Cup. Officially, the Stade Colombes held 60,000. England proved a popular draw. Bert, Stan and the entire England party left Paris relieved that their fraught European tour was over. It was supposed to be in some respects a holiday and their critics thought so. However, it turned out to be anything but a holiday.

Jules Rimet even suggested that England might host the 1942 World Cup despite not being FIFA members. The idea was given 'widespread support' from other competing nations at the World Cup in France. But Rimet also admitted that Germany had a 'prior right' to the 1942 tournament after turning down the chance to host the 1938 World Cup. Perhaps the Nazis had an alternative sporting propaganda coup in mind after their Olympic 'triumph' a couple of years earlier. England, the father of the world game, were never going to turn up at FIFA's World Cup out of insular hubris and snobbery.

At the World Cup, Germany suffered the humiliation of being knocked out in the opening round by Switzerland after a replay, the Swiss winning 4-2. Italy's political soldiers held on to their world title in Paris, beating Hungary 4-2 in the final. They were regularly booed by the French crowd for making the fascist salute. The hosting of the 1942 World Cup turned out to be academic. There was not to be another tournament until 1950.

Bert returned home to Sandbach to play cricket and was uncertain about his club future. His club manager Billy Hampton, no doubt, tried to reassure him during England's trip to Berlin. But his days at Leeds were over. Tottenham Hotspur wanted to regain its status as one of the top clubs in the land, having languished in the second division of the Football League. The club's new manager, Peter McWilliams, declared that there was no shortage of money. There was one snag – a shortage of top-class players wanting to drop out of the first division.

Clifford Webb wrote in the *Daily Herald*, 'He [McWilliams] assures me that money is no object; that Tottenham are going after nothing less than top-notchers in their effort to regain first division status. But he is equally emphatic that never, in his long football career, has he known such a shortage of star players. Clubs fortunate enough to possess the outstanding players have refused to be tempted by large-sized cheques.'

One exception just happened to be cash-strapped Leeds. Bert sat at home in Sandbach on 15 June 1938 waiting for a knock on the door. He suspected that Leeds might sell him despite the objections of his manager, Billy Hampson. A telegram boy delivered the message summoning him to Elland Road. He was to go there to meet the Spurs boss, Peter McWilliams, to sign the transfer forms. The boy from a quiet town in rural Cheshire contemplated life in the London metropolis. Just as importantly, he considered life as a professional footballer at a lower level.

Bert preferred not to venture south. Just stay north of the River Trent. To Bert, London might as well have been a foreign country, rather than England's capital city. But did he have a choice? Once an offer came in for him from one of the capital's clubs he was in no position to refuse. Leeds United were skint.

Footballers back in the 1930s were more or less club property. Describing them as mere commercial or playing assets might be a tad generous. Critics described their terms of employment as medieval, a form of servitude.

'Money matters in football,' Bert's mate Stanley Matthews always told him. Forget just a knock-about in the park. Forget morality or ethics. 'Was football a sport?' No longer. Long before the advent of England's Premier League, disgruntled professional footballers resentfully recognised that their sport had grown into a ruthless business. Many wanted their cut of the riches collected at the turnstiles. Stanley Matthews turned out to be a recalcitrant football rebel. He also enjoyed hero status among fans.

As the 1937/38 season drew to a close, Matthews put in a transfer request. Stoke City fans reacted with fury, blaming both club and player. Thousands attended a protest meeting at the King's Hall in Stoke. Matthews backed down. Hero status among his hometown fans mattered, at least for the time being. His mate

Bert less so. Hero or rebel? Maybe both? No, just another England footballer. Talented but not one to build cult status. He had his views on the game and he did as he was told.

The bright lights of London beckoned. 'It is a good transfer fee,' he would tell his alarmed mother, Alice. 'I'll get a cut of the fee. At least, I hope so.' Nothing was certain when it came to dealing with the butchers, the bakers and candlestick makers running pre-war English football. As it turned out, Alice Sproston operated quite shrewdly on behalf of her son.

Leeds United sold Bert Sproston for a club record of between £8,000 and £10,000 to Tottenham Hotspur. The *Yorkshire Post* commented, 'The departure of Sproston will be a big loss to United, but a club of their limited financial resources could not decline such an offer.' It added, 'He has been a model player, both on and off the field, during the whole of his career with Leeds United.' During his five-year Leeds career he developed into one of the country's 'most speedy' players and had 'developed the constructive side of his high game to a high pitch or proficiency'.

Fans expressed their outrage in the letters' pages of the *Yorkshire Post*. 'Once again we have the old, old story from Leeds United,' wrote one fan. 'This time it's Sproston, a worthy addition to the ranks of first-class men, who have been found to be superfluous by the officials at Elland Road. With monotonous regularity we have been promised great things from our team, such slogans as "This is United's Year" being glibly circulated. Last year we had a team of more than usual promise, and promptly, efficiently, and characteristically, the directors make a mess of it. Sproston was one of the mainstays of the side, and I, for one, am determined not to support a soccer team, whose management pursues such a short-sighted, money-grabbing policy.'

Another fan joined in, 'Sir – In reference to the transfer of Bert Sproston, I think the Leeds United directors made the biggest mistake of their lives. Bert, as we all know, was the mainstay of the team. Probably the directors think they have done themselves a good turn by collecting nearly £10,000; but I can assure you they have not. Instead of United building up a young team that would play real good football, they get a good man and transfer him instead of building up a team around him. Leeds will never get a good team, never get good gates if this kind of carrying-on is going to be allowed.'

Leeds United's 'glory days' just happened to be some decades off. Many Leeds fans of the 1930s accepted the need to sell Sproston. After all, full-back was hardly a position to build a team around. It was also a decent amount of money for a defender and they wished Sproston well.

Another fan wrote to the *Yorkshire Evening Post*, 'Sproston's transfer can be made a good piece of business. It must be remembered that although he is an outstanding player, right-back is hardly a key position, and when he was out of the side last season there was no appreciable difference in the effectiveness of the team.'

Sproston might be forgiven for thinking that giving up top-flight football as an England international was a mistake. He had struggled to win a regular England place. It was only in the past 12 months that he had made the breakthrough, seeing off Arsenal's George Male.

The gap between the first division and the second division of the old Football League was nowhere near as great as between the Premier League and Championship in modern football. Nevertheless, he risked losing his England place, albeit while playing for a high-profile club in the capital.

The England defender appeared keen to justify the decision to drop down into the second division. He set out his views in a syndicated preview of the 1938/39 season for regional newspapers. At no point does he admit that he had no choice but to go. Tottenham put in a bid. Leeds accepted the bid. The player, in this case Sproston, was sold. Forget any hint of enthusiasm for the move. It was merely practical, a necessity for both clubs.

'In moving from Leeds United to the Spurs, I was, in a sense, making a drop in status, but I did not look at the matter in such a light,' Sproston said. 'Not that, in the first place, I had any particular desire to come to Tottenham, or to London at all. I had only played on the Spurs ground twice, once in a representative match. During the latter part of last season, I somehow got the impression that Leeds United were not particularly keen to keep me. Hence when the suggestion was put that I should be transferred, I was quite willing to fall in with the idea.'

As for dropping down a division, Sproston declared, 'It has ceased to be a tremendous calamity for a club to drop out of the top class and into the second section.' He took comfort in the large attendances. 'The figures do show the way the wind is blowing: point to the fact that the second division is now such in little more than name.' He added, 'The Spurs will have serious rivals in the come-back struggle. It is difficult to imagine that Manchester City, having had the unique experience of being first division champions one season and relegated the next, will be content with a place among the second class. They got some new players last season who are good, and who are sure to be concerned in the effort to get back.'

Little did Sproston realise but he would end up at Manchester City within months. Then again, his lukewarm comments on arriving at White Hart Lane offered a clue that he might not stay long in north London. His one experience of top-class action with Spurs just happened to be a friendly – a pre-season north London derby against Arsenal at Highbury. More than 40,000 fans turned up with only local bragging rights at stake for bitter rivals enjoying contrasting fortunes. Arsenal were champions of England while Tottenham were no longer one of the country's top clubs. Profits from the game went to charity, the King George V Jubilee Trust Fund. Friendly matches across the country contributed more than £22,000 (roughly £1.25m, allowing for inflation) to the fund's pot. Almost £3,000 was raised at Highbury alone.

Just to add a little spice to theoretically a friendly match for charity, Arsenal signed a player targeted all summer by Spurs. After signing Sproston back in June, Peter McWilliams spent a week trying to lure Welsh international Bryn Jones away from Wolverhampton Wanderers. Spurs put in a bid of £14,000 and McWilliams was given permission to talk to Jones. Unlike Sproston, Jones opted to stay at his club. There was no pressure on him to leave. Wolves were a financially sound football club. They were ambitious, league runners-up in season 1937/38. Arsenal won the title and the Gunners then targeted Jones.

Arsenal paid the money for Jones instead of Spurs. Jones was unable to resist the temptation of signing for the league champions. He agreed to the move. There was to be no drop in league status.

What would happen in the pre-season north London derby? Highbury was packed. Sproston's battle with Cliff Bastin and Bryn Jones on the right side of the Arsenal attack provided an intriguing sub-plot to the match. Just for added interest, Sproston's rival for the England right-back spot, George Male, had recovered from injury.

Spurs won the match 2-0. Sproston won his personal battles with England team-mate Bastin and Wales' inside-forward Jones. Fleet Street football writers hailed him as the star of the show. 'Sproston took the honours' proclaimed the *Daily Herald*. 'Sproston is in a class by himself, and the excellence of his positioning in the game allowed neither Bastin nor Bryn Jones to take liberties, even if they were playing at half speed.'

Stanley Halsey of the *Daily Express* called Sproston's performance 'superb'. Roy Horobin of *Reynolds News* wrote, 'Friendly or no friendly, you can't make a parlour game out of a Spurs and Arsenal match. It is no use attempting to describe this as a practice match. Right from the first foul – just about five seconds after the kick-off – it was a north London battle.'

Horobin singled out Sproston as the 'star turn', commenting, 'For a long time it has been a toss-up whether he [Sproston] or Male is the best right-back in the country, and after this I think Sproston is still just a short head in front. I am sure he is going to prove the finest bargain the Spurs have made in years.'

J.G. Orange of London's *Evening News* also praised Spurs' manager for a sound piece of transfer business. He wrote, 'I doubt whether a better back has come to London than Sproston, formerly of Leeds who is now on the Tottenham Hotspur staff. Sproston was the first player signed by Mr Peter McWilliams on his return to Tottenham. Incidentally, I believe the Spurs will benefit more from the return of Peter McWilliams to manage the side than from the arrival of half a dozen stars.'

After the game Bryn Jones said, 'I must admit that I am not sorry that Bert is not playing against us on Saturday, for he is always a very difficult man to pass.' The pair struck up an unlikely friendship, even travelling together from London as playing rivals for Wales' game against England in Cardiff.

Sproston's place in the England side looked safe. A long and successful playing career awaited a 23-year-old footballer. It was not to be. During September 1938, the British prime minister, Neville Chamberlain, proclaimed 'peace for our time' as he arrived from Germany by air after talks with Hitler. There was to be no peace. War was to intervene. Ensuring one Jewish citizen arrived safely from Germany to England became Bert Sproston's immediate priority, rather than his football career.

Meantime, Bert needed to sort out not only some tickets for a Jewish refugee, but a UK visa for him to travel from Nazi Germany to England. Would Bert have contemplated the looming threat of world war as he returned to his north London digs? No other England footballer, not even his mate Stanley Matthews who joined him on a sightseeing tour of Berlin, was in a better position to assess the dire nature of the Nazi threat. Bert received first-hand accounts posted from a lonely teenager in Berlin. Rolf just left out the painful bits, the growing psychological trauma. But his distress was clear. Regular missives arrived by post in the fan mail at White Hart Lane. Rolf's need for help was escalating quickly.

His transfer to Tottenham Hotspur had gone ahead in June 1938 for what turned out to be a brief, unhappy spell at the club. But Sproston took the opportunity to put an unusual request to his new bosses. He wanted them to sponsor a visa for Rolf to make the journey to London for the game between England and a Europe XI. Quite whether Spurs' links to London's Jewish community were helpful is open to conjecture.

Spurs had understandably been criticised by British Jewish leaders for hosting Germany in December 1935, the Nazi swastika flying above White Hart Lane. Perhaps for Tottenham Hotspur Football Club it was time to make amends. But Rolf's family believe that Sproston did most of the challenging work to help him, rather than the football club. Sadly, Spurs, while extremely co-operative with my enquiries, have no formal record of the efforts to grant this German-Jewish fan a UK visa. If anything, the FA in a rare, enlightened act for a sports governing body of the time co-operated. Stanley Rous responded positively to Sproston's entreaties.

Rolf's son Alan Freeman said, 'It was Sproston himself who took matters at hand. He took it up with the English Football Association. I have to presume the FA in turn asked for the visa to be issued. By then Bert was a Spurs player who also got the club to host him [Rolf] for the first few days after his arrival at Liverpool Street by way of Harwich. From that moment onwards my dad was a lifetime Spurs supporter and friend of Bert Sproston until the day he died.' Spurs signed a new player, an England international. The club also had a new fan, a German-Jewish refugee from Berlin. He just needed to venture from the Nazi German capital to London.

AUF WIEDERSEHEN BERLIN

SO DIFFICULT to sleep, all Rolf heard was the slow ticking of his alarm clock. For once all of Berlin, a bustling and once scandalously decadent city under Germany's Weimar Republic, seemed asleep. Across Germany the peace of so many was shattered over the past few years by the thud of jackboots and the battering of batons on doors. Nazi victims hid indoors, beaten on the streets if they ventured outdoors.

Rolf gripped his pillow, gazed vacantly at the window curtains as dawn began to break. He was not going to cower under the Nazi iron rule. One day they would be cowering before him. Unlike them, he genuinely embraced joy through sport. There was a football fixture to fulfil. His time had arrived and the alarm clock rang. It was time to leave Berlin. His refugee journey began.

Just one formality remained. He needed his visa for travel to England. Rolf, in plain sight of prying Nazis eyes, joined the queues of people snaking along from the British embassy, the Palais Strousberg on Wilhelmstrasse. Little hope of those poor souls avoiding attention as they sought to leave Germany, hopefully to the embrace of their Anglo-Saxon cousins in England. Hitler's chancellery also stood proudly on Wilhelmstrasse. His new palace was still being built. Hundreds of Hitler's devotees, his cult followers, held a daily vigil along the street. So did the SS, the Gestapo, even traffic cops owing full allegiance to the Führer.

Britain's ambassador to Berlin, Sir Nevile Henderson, wanted a move to a slightly less prominent location. His bosses back in London refused. Vanity prevented them from giving up a prestige property that their Victorian predecessors picked up for a bargain from a failed German railway magnate. More importantly, it was the least of priorities amid deteriorating diplomatic relations with Germany.

Just popping along to check on his visa application put Rolf at risk but it was one worth taking. After all, he was just a football fan. Who might spot an ulterior motive? For the Nazis, nothing escaped their attention. He left the opportunity to go to the British embassy to collect his visa until the last minute. Any later, he would miss the game in London.

Rolf knocked his alarm clock on the head. Looked at it, just to double-check the time, and chucked it into his flimsy suitcase. The mornings in late October gradually drew shorter – darkness descending day by day in Berlin and London. He needed the alarm clock for the trip to London. An afternoon kick-off but he wanted to be up early on the morning of the match. There was just the small matter of getting to the British capital in the first place.

Sipping a cup of rough coffee, Rolf checked his luggage, the sparse collection of photos as mementos of life growing up in Berlin. Along with these precious items to help lodge memories of happier times in Berlin, he placed more prosaic items, tickets for the boat train among them, into his suitcase. Time to pick up the visa. Rolf stood up, buttoned up his coat, opened the door, switched off the light and stepped out into the dim light on Kirchstrasse in the central Berlin district of Moabit. His journey to freedom had begun.

Arriving on Wilhelmstrasse, he only noticed a few of Hitler's fanatical stragglers holding vigil outside the chancellery. Guards kept watch on them and the visitors to the British embassy began their daily queue. Rolf took his place. It was 25 October 1938. England were due to play the Rest of Europe the next day at Highbury in north London. He waited patiently for an hour or so, then came the invitation to go into the passport office.

Entreaties from England international, Bert Sproston, worked. Former public schoolboys set up the Football Association, just some 75 years earlier. Ostensibly Rolf was off to help celebrate the anniversary of the occasion. The sport founded by a group of gentlemen in the Freemasons' Tavern just off Covent Garden in central London had been transformed. It was no longer a posh sport for old public school pupils. It was an international sport, for the masses. A working-class kid from Sandbach, much to his own surprise, pulled off a diplomatic coup. To be fair, it was a rarity.

Rolf was one of football's devotees. His race, his religion ensured that Germany's rulers made it difficult, if not impossible, to play the world's most popular team sport. They ignored, at least for the time being, exclusively Jewish clubs in Berlin. Those would inevitably come under threat. No more staging of the Olympics or other international events to con the world. The populist politics of the Nazis ensured that they had already manipulated football, all sport, for their own nefarious purposes on the world stage.

As a casualty of the British establishment's naivety, England defender Bert Sproston impressed the posh boys still running the sport in his country. As one of the Nazi-saluting England players from that infamous match in the spring of 1938, Bert did his 'bit' for British diplomacy. Rugby just happened to be the posh boys' sport, football for the elite of society. Just as a stroke of luck, some of them still adopted a fondness for the gentlemen's sport played by hooligans. Yes, he played soccer. But Bert was no hooligan, nor his prospective refugee.

Rolf Friedland (later to be known as Ralph Freeman) spoke to the historian Helen Fry with his wife Eva for her book, *Jews in North Devon During the Second World War*. He told Helen that he regularly corresponded with Bert. Rolf's letters arrived in the post room at Elland Road, a rare German supporter sending in fan mail. The German-stamped letters were addressed to Mr B. Sproston c/o Leeds United AFC, Elland Road, Leeds, England. No secret code in the letter itself for suspicious Gestapo operatives to decipher. Just in plain English, likely dictated to Rolf by someone with a better command of the language from one of Berlin's Jewish support groups. His plans were no secret. To any prying eyes, there was just a bizarre obsession with an English football club and its star defender.

Leeds would lose their German fan once Bert Sproston went on his way to Tottenham Hotspur. Instead, Rolf's letters were redirected to Mr B. Sproston c/o Tottenham Hotspur FC, White Hart Lane, London, England. Every time, Bert wrote back offering reassurance. He had arranged for the Football Association to send a personal invitation to Rolf to attend the England versus the Rest of Europe match. Much to Rolf's relief and excitement, the invite arrived at his Berlin flat. As a result, the British embassy in Berlin granted Rolf a visa to travel to England. Helen Fry commented, 'Bert Sproston was thus instrumental in saving Rolf's life.'

After the intervention of Bert and the FA, the passport officer at the British embassy in Berlin gazed at Rolf before stamping his visa. He made a cursory inspection of the bold German teenager's papers. These included a letter on FA-headed notepaper inviting him to attend the England v Rest of Europe game at Highbury. Another letter, this time written on Tottenham Hotspur FC-headed notepaper, was from its full-back, Bert Sproston. He looked forward to being reunited with Rolf at the game. The officer reached for the ink stamp. The visa was issued for on or about Wednesday, 26 October 1938, the date of the England versus the Rest of Europe game.

To the British he was just another football fan, albeit one with impressive references. Those involved in the issuing of the visa maybe just did not realise that he was also intent on becoming a refugee. But they more than likely guessed it was a possibility. His claim for political asylum would be made once safely on English soil. The game at Highbury, of course, was to come first.

Just why did Rolf need a visa? Back in the 1930s, they were not quite as common as decades later, not even for travel between democratic and totalitarian states. Strict visa requirements for German and Austrian visitors to Britain only came into force just a week or so after England's game with Germany in Berlin. Up until spring 1938, immigration controls between Britain and Germany did not match the future European Union's free movement of labour but were fairly relaxed.

There were a couple of important conditions. Nazis controlled who might leave Germany. Its legions of football fans happily travelled to London and Glasgow, then back to Germany again, under the 'Strength through Joy' programme. More sinisterly, the Nazis pursued a policy throughout the 1930s infamously known in German as *judenrein* (cleansed of Jews). German Jews were allowed to leave, effectively driven out into neighbouring countries. (This was before they turned to murdering Jews on an industrial scale, in their millions.)

Britain's immigration policy of the 1930s tended to favour wealthier Germans, those able to support themselves and find a job. Unfortunately, shop workers need not apply. Nor, oddly, did many doctors and dentists, thanks to opposition from the British Medical Association and British Dental Association. Britain's agriculture and horticulture sector welcomed immigrant workers.

On 25 April 1938, the British ambassador, Sir Nevile Henderson, informed the Nazis that his government would now insist on immigrants to Britain having a visa. The Nazis naturally objected to the new policy. It made their unofficial expulsion of Jews more difficult. It also, of course, made life for Rolf and tens of thousands more German Jews even more perilous, so he had to come up with a plan to get a visa, and quite implausibly turned to the England football team for help.

The home secretary, Sir Samuel Hoare, confirmed details of the new immigration restrictions for Germans and Austrians in a Commons statement on 3 May 1938. They would come into force from 21 May 1938. According to Sir Samuel, this was done to make it easier to administer the UK's asylum system. He stated it applied to persons, 'who for political, racial or religious reasons had to leave their own country'. He further commented, 'It was impossible to admit indiscriminately all persons claiming to be refugees, and if would-be immigrants were to arrive in large numbers, without any preliminary examination, great difficulty would be created at the ports and unnecessary hardship might be inflicted on applicants whom it might be found necessary to reject.'

Critics objected but the UK government ignored their concerns. Sir Samuel went as far as telling the Board of Deputies of British

Jews, 'With all the sympathy in the world it would not be right to overlook the position of our own labour market.'

Rolf Friedland's visa application stated that he simply wanted to go to England to watch a football match – rather than making a permanent move which would involve him needing a place to live and a job. He figured he would then take his chances and stay in England.

From the British embassy in Berlin, it was just a 15-minute walk to the railway station adjacent to the city's zoo. The guards outside Hitler's chancellery watched him go by. He was no loss to them. From the relative calm of Berlin's early morning streets, Rolf walked into Berlin Zoologischer Garten station. War seemed a long way off as 'normal' life unfolded before his eyes, commuters rushing about. They mixed with international passengers as they made their way for points north, south, east and west. For Rolf, west was best.

His passenger train, his own personal football special, stood at the platform, steam gently oozing from its engine. It was about to leave Berlin, bound for the Hook of Holland. A porter blew his whistle with a loud shrill. The train crew fired up the engine. Bahnhof Berlin was enveloped in steam. The train's whistle blew as the brakes were released. Slowly but surely the wheels ground into action. It was not a football special in any conventional sense, certainly not on a par with trains taking German fans to Berlin for an international between Germany and England some months earlier.

More men in Nazi uniform strutted along the platform. They also gathered on the train. British footballers going to Nazi Germany, ever since the visit of Derby County in the summer of 1934, had noted the penchant for German men and boys to dress up in paramilitary style uniforms. The Nazi outfits boosted fragile male egos. They were also meant to intimidate. On board the train sat the nervous refugee, Rolf Friedland, clutching his remarkable piece of memorabilia. It was secured after his entreaties to a random England footballer at Berlin's Olympiastadion back in May.

Rather than being destined to travel on one of Hitler's 'death trains' during the war, Rolf began a life-saving journey by rail. His train eased out of Berlin, leaving behind a thriving metropolis adorned with the symbols of fascism. Gathering speed across the Prussian countryside, it eventually steamed into the relative safety of the Benelux countries. There, Rolf was free of men in Nazi uniform with prying eyes and suspicious ears. If he felt an immense sense of relief, it was understandable but his adventure was far from over.

From the Hook of Holland, he boarded the ferry for Harwich on the Essex coast. Nobody stopped him. British immigration officials waved through the nervous teenager at Harwich. Safely on English soil, he took another train, heading for Liverpool Street Station in London. From there, he was reunited with his father, Adalbert, who lived on New Cavendish Street, but there was no room to stay at his dad's flat.

According to Rolf's future wife Eva, he endured an 'ambivalent' relationship with his parents. She put this down to his early years spent at a Bavarian children's home for hyper-active infants, then boarding school. Mr and Mrs Friedland were unable to cope. A loving bond endured but Rolf became independent. He was not going to rely on his estranged parents. He chose not to see his mother, living more than 30 miles away in Guildford, Surrey. He was once again living in the same country as his parents. A new life in England awaited. He was still on his own.

After his brief reunion with his dad, he checked the directions for his final destination – Tottenham Hotspur's football ground. Apparently thanks to Sproston, he spent his first three nights in England as a refugee sleeping in the dressing rooms there. The head groundsman at Spurs, William Over, was waiting for Bert's guest.

The player himself was ensconced in the England team hotel on the outskirts of London. Rolf was shown to the White Hart Lane dressing rooms. Mr Over, whose father John found fame as the groundsman at both the Oval cricket ground and White Hart Lane, dealt with some unusual requests in his time at Tottenham Hotspur but this was the oddest. Mr Over was happy to help the German refugee.

On the morning of the game between England and the Rest of Europe, Rolf woke in his unfamiliar surroundings – the dressing room of an English football club. He helped himself to the large bath, a dream fulfilled for any aspiring footballer. Just a couple of notes to pick up from the reliable Mr Over. One was in an official envelope from the FA, a ticket for the game. Just the invitation to attend the game was sent to Rolf's home in Berlin. Clearly, the visa had been granted to travel to the UK. All he needed was the matchday ticket. The other was a letter from Bert Sproston. It gave the address of his digs in north London and rather surprisingly his parents in Sandbach, Cheshire. Rolf had barely heard of the place – English geography was a mystery to him.

He then set off, with directions, for the famous Highbury Stadium, home of Tottenham's great rivals, Arsenal. Once again, the Gunners were staging a fixture at Highbury, replete with political and diplomatic overtones. No 'Battle of Highbury' this time around – just a birthday celebration, one proving that football can be a force for peace. The guest of honour was the Duke of Kent – the king's brother. Bert Sproston invited his own guest of honour – a refugee from Nazi tyranny.

ENGLAND V EUROPE

ROLF WAS safe. Just how to move him from the temporary hospitality of Tottenham Hotspur posed the next problem. Perhaps the FA might put him up in the England team hotel? Maybe allow him to feast on the rich food available – the fine fare that snobbish Fleet Street writers considered to be inappropriate for working-class lads? Not even worth considering such a fanciful notion, Bert knew the answer would be an emphatic no.

For a glorified exhibition game, the holiday atmosphere so derided by the players' critics neatly suited their training camp. Golf at the Bushey Hall Hotel in Hertfordshire filled the time in between fitness sessions at Highbury. Bert went around the course in a foursome with Stanley Matthews, Frank Broome and Willie Hall. They played for fun, despite the fierce competitive nature in all of them. They happily joined in with the obligatory photo opportunity, dressed as if they were playing a round at The Open golf championship, rather than a hotel leisure course.

It was best just to pose for photos rather than take journalists' questions. The newspapers made for grim reading. The games in Berlin and Paris aside, England's form was poor. A shock 4-2 defeat to Wales at Ninian Park in Cardiff on Saturday, 22 October 1938 angered fans. Bert Sproston suffered some polite but stinging criticism in the press along with most of the rest of the team. He travelled to the game with Arsenal's Bryn Jones. The Welsh winger was on this occasion happy to play against him. Only Matthews enjoyed some praise.

The *Daily Express* accused the England defenders of cracking under pressure from the Welsh forwards. Clifford Webb of the *Daily Herald* commented, 'Sproston's lapses at Cardiff looked bad.' Webb questioned whether Sproston would be able to cope with the best of European wingers. He added, 'Yet it is so rarely that Sproston has an indifferent match that it is conceivable he will be back to his best at Highbury [against a rest of Europe XI].'

A German journalist watching the game remarked that he was staggered by England's lack of teamwork compared with the team's performance against Germany earlier in the year. As a result of the defeat, the FA's selectors met in Cardiff City's boardroom to reconsider the England team's line-up for the game at Highbury. They confidently asserted before the defeat to Wales that the team would be unchanged for the European challenge. Instead, they made changes. Wolves's Stan Cullis was brought back into the side to bolster the defence. He replaced Alf Young of Huddersfield Town. Willie Hall replaced Sheffield Wednesday's Jackie Robinson, one of the goalscorers from England's 6-3 defeat of Germany.

It was important to drum up publicity for the game. Tickets were being sold at a snail's pace. Rolf Friedland was happy, as he settled in at White Hart Lane, with a ticket for the game. A job and a permanent home in England needed to wait. The FA did help Bert Sproston to secure Rolf a UK visa. The matchday ticket was therefore never a problem, just a minor technicality. Selling them to disgruntled English fans for an exhibition game after defeat to Wales was another matter.

Just as a reminder, the FA first proposed the England versus the Rest of Europe game back on 30 April 1938, the date it named the England team to play Germany in Berlin on 14 May 1938. It was meant to be an 'attraction' to form part of the FA's 75th anniversary celebrations. Football had firmly established itself as the world's most popular team sport but for this exhibition game there was a distinct lack of enthusiasm. Even the formal announcement of the fixture at the FA's summer meeting in Scarborough was overshadowed by a radical and controversial innovation. Difficult to believe in the modern era but numbering players' shirts provoked controversy. Traditionalists at the FA had rejected such a 'continental' notion, foreigners interfering with their sport. But to much surprise, a proposal to number players' shirts was accepted. It was put forward bizarrely by New Zealand's representative on the FA council, Brigadier General W.R.N. Maddox. Players would be numbered 1 to 10 with the goalkeeper wearing no number.

The Scottish FA (SFA) rejected the idea. It wrongly assumed that England's FA might do the same. *The Scotsman* noted that England's FA had 'defied' the SFA. Aston Villa's chairman and FA vice-president, Frederick Rinder, commented, 'I can see no logical objection to the idea. The England team will be numbered against Scotland. Objections arise from old-fashioned sentiment and the present tendency of interchange of positions calls for numbering to assist even the experienced spectator to identify players. I have always been in favour of numbering.' Teams would also wear numbers in the FA Cup Final and semi-finals.

Final details of the game between England and the Rest of Europe were also released at the FA's summer meeting. The game was to be held at Highbury. Critics thought that Wembley would have been a better venue for a 'showpiece' event. Once it became difficult to sell tickets, such criticism disappeared. A half-empty Wembley would be embarrassing for the FA. As for shirts, FIFA made it clear that its Europe team would wear numbers on the back. Hard to dismiss the idea that the FA decided to follow suit.

Naturally once the fuss died down over the numbering of players' shirts, much hype surrounded the clash between England and the best players from the European mainland. It was largely political in nature and came from national newspapers supporting appeasement. Editorials in British newspapers stressed the importance of the game in the cause of peace.

The *Daily Mirror* wondered whether the German and Italian players would be forced to play in a pure Aryan manner, captained dictatorially. It questioned whether they would achieve sufficient teamwork with forwards from the democracies of Belgium and Norway. Then it unhelpfully commented, 'It will be seen (later) whether, if the dictated players lose, they will be concentrated in camps or beheaded on their return to their respective countries.' The *Daily Mirror* meant it as a joke. Awfully, a similar fate awaited young Rolf Friedland if he returned to Germany, regardless of something as trivial as the result of a football match.

The Times emphasised the opportunity to build friendly international relations. It even ventured to suggest that the name of the sport, association football, was inherently friendly. *The Times* commented, 'There are indeed footballers and other athletes of experience who wonder whether international contests do not rather inflame rather than allay international jealousy. Yet few will be able to watch or read of today's game without giving it a place above the usual run of such encounters and without finding that their thoughts have strayed wishfully to international association on another plane where the game might also be greater than the player of the game and the run of play equally obedient to the referee's whistle.'

Charles Buchan focused on the Englishman abroad or as he quaintly put it, 'the Britisher'. Buchan reflected, 'Britishers on the continent will be eagerly awaiting the result at Highbury between England and Rest of Europe. It means a lot to them from the point of view of prestige. I do not mean that the result will be an event of world-wide importance or that defeat will be a shattering blow to England. But a victory would make the lot of the Britishers abroad much happier.'

Rous promoted the idea of the England versus Rest of Europe match in the interest of furthering international relations. Specifically, his grandiose idea was to repair British football's broken ties with FIFA, even open talks to rejoin the sport's world governing body. It also served his personal ambitions quite well. Rous eventually ended up as FIFA president. Rolf Friedland harboured in his own mind a better idea – he wanted an invitation to the game as an escape route.

Once again, the FA chose to dabble in international political relations. No lessons had been learnt from a chastening weekend in Berlin for English football. The FA, British government ministers, and the sympathetic right-wing press all appeared ludicrously proud of the Nazi salute given by England's international footballers.

The flags of all the nations represented in the Rest of Europe team were due to adorn Highbury. These included the Nazi flag of Germany. A couple of German players, Andreas Kupfer and Albin Kitzinger, turned out for the Rest of Europe. Just Britain's Union flag and the FIFA flag flew instead.

Most of the European players came from the world champions, Italy. Commendatore Vittorio Pozzo returned to the scene of the

'Battle of Highbury', this time as the Europe manager. Quite bizarrely, Italian radio pulled its planned live broadcast of the game. A team of five employees of Ente Italiano per le Audizioni Radiofoniche (EIAR) turned up at Highbury with their equipment. Benito Mussolini's fascist government informed them that it had cancelled the broadcast and no reason was given. The British press speculated that Mussolini feared a crushing defeat for the European team.

Undeterred, Pozzo indulged in some boxing-style pre-match trash-talk to wind up his English hosts. 'English football is on the decline,' Pozzo said. 'I also believe that the intellectual level of the English players has definitely fallen. There are few players in Britain with whom one can discuss the subject of football. English football is no longer what it used to be. It is no longer the football of artists.'

Fog hanging over London hardly lifted the mood of the players and staff of both sides. Sproston and the rest of the England squad were relieved to return to their hotel in Bushey. It was bathed in clear wintry sunshine in contrast to the fogbound conditions for a training session at Highbury. The European team trained at Stamford Bridge in the morning. They then crossed London to familiarise themselves with Highbury. Arsenal's manager, George Allison, turned up to welcome them. He also turned on the newly installed floodlights to help lift the gloom.

Disgruntled British football writers moaned about the numbering of shirts, an unwelcome novelty. It was deemed a failure for the game between Wales and England. The numbers of the players on the field did not correspond with those published in the matchday programme. Bert Sproston picked the England number 2 shirt off his peg. The programme put him down as number 1 on the England team. The Football Association of Wales followed the protocol deemed necessary by their English counterparts. No numbers for goalkeepers, the rest 1 to 10. Unfortunately, on matchday the English kit manager decided otherwise. Hence, the frustration and amusement, rather than confusion for fans consulting their programmes.

The much-heralded game between England and the best of the Rest of Europe could offer turned out to be something of a flop. Predictions of record-breaking gate receipts proved well off the mark. The young refugee was keen to watch the game, but his enthusiasm was not quite shared by the average English football fan living in London.

After England's 4-2 defeat in Cardiff to Wales, perhaps they were not too keen on the rationale behind the game. Stanley Rous of the FA openly admitted that the gate money went towards a celebratory banquet at a plush London hotel. Grassroots football, the clubs founding the game in a London pub, lost out. Football fans cared little for Rous's lofty personal ambitions. The patrician leader of the FA appeared not to care.

One thing was for sure, the game turned out to be less than competitive. The absent fans made the right choice. A full-strength England side won comfortably 3-0 and it could have been more. Tottenham's Willie Hall opened the scoring for England after a pass from Matthews. Tommy Lawton scored the second in a goalmouth scramble. Len Goulden finished off the scoring with a rasping left-foot shot just inside the post.

Clifford Webb of the *Daily Herald* dismissed the game as 'rather a dull business'. Before the match he had expected it to be played in a 'carnival spirit' despite the dominance of the Italian contingent. England's goalkeeper, Vic Woodley, was unemployed as Sproston, Cullis and Hapgood easily dealt with the European forwards.

John Thompson of the *Daily Mirror* merely described the match as one of the politest he had seen. It justified his newspaper's editorial comment that, 'sport makes for peace'. Commenting on the disappointing crowd of 40,185, well below the Highbury capacity of the day, the *Mirror* man blamed the cost of tickets. Admission prices ranged from 2 shillings to 21 shillings (from £5 to £55 in today's money, taking into account inflation). It led to a familiar criticism that ordinary fans were being priced out of the working-class game of football. As for the players, England's captain Eddie Hapgood simply commented, 'It was a fine sporting game, and we thoroughly enjoyed it.' Europe's captain, Raymond Braine of Belgium responded, 'England well deserved to win. They were faster and stronger than we were, and their positional play was better than ours.'

John MacAdam of the *Daily Express* complained that it was impossible to form any estimate of the real worth of either team. As it was an exhibition game with the Europeans fielding a scratch side, this seemed to miss the point but he did concede that both teams offered up a delightful exhibition of football. Sproston and the rest of the England team were not tested. It was a mystery that England only scored three goals.

Charles Buchan wrote, 'As the big birthday show of the Football Association it fell a long way below expectations. Big blocks of empty seats in the Highbury Hill stand added to the general atmosphere of disappointment.' English imagination appeared to be sadly lacking. The European team's deficiencies became only too obvious. As for Sproston's performance? Hapgood enjoyed the better game at full-back while appearing vulnerable as the Europeans counter-attacked. He felt both full-backs were able to cover any defensive gaps as their team-mates attacked what he tellingly for the time called the 'European Maginot Line'.

Hopefully, Rolf enjoyed the game more than the distinguished former English international. He did not feel the need to resort to military references in assessing a game of football. He knew all too well the dangers of militarisation in society. Buchan, even after the subsequent world war, saw no problem in England players making a Nazi salute before a game, being out of touch with reality on the issue.

One cutting criticism was of the England selectors. Argus for the British regional newspapers observed, 'The tragedy to me was the England international selection committee. One respects old age, but as they came out of the cars to enter the Arsenal ground, some having to be helped up the steps – well, I thought it's time some of them realised that there comes a time when a young man should take over.' The one England player that Argus criticised was Bert Sproston. 'Sproston, in my judgement, was not the back we saw at Leeds.'

The great and the good of European football accepted their invites to the post-match banquet, including the FIFA president, Jules Rimet. A future FIFA boss felt satisfied by the day's events – he was, of course, Stanley Rous. He reflected, 'If the match did nothing to make us aware of the dangers of being so inward-looking, the occasion at least helped those of us who were seeking an opportunity to bring the British Associations back within FIFA. Friendships were cemented.'

One young German-Jewish fan avoided the ignominy of effectively helping to pay for the dinner and champagne of the German delegates present at the banquet. Sproston had managed to reserve him a complimentary ticket. The FA just posted it care of Mr Over at Tottenham Hotspur FC. Unlike most of the fans present at Highbury, Rolf left the ground feeling happy. He faced a much greater challenge than suffering 90 minutes of a dull game of exhibition football. He needed digs and a job.

Sproston's faltering form caused him concern. Maybe it was time to leave London? As a quandary, it seemed almost ridiculous. The footballer and the refugee both faced an uncertain future but for contrasting reasons. Bert's problems as an unhappy footballer paled by comparison with the challenges facing Rolf.

The German teenager's UK visa was due to run out. Conditions in Germany took a severe turn for the worse. His visa's expiry date? On or about 9 November 1938, *Kristallnacht*. A horrified world awoke realising it was on the brink of war. Nazi salutes by England footballers in an act of appeasement appeared futile. So did staging matches at Highbury in the hope of furthering peace between nations. Rolf could be forgiven for offering such advice to the FA bosses as he gratefully picked up his visa for freedom.

BLOOMSBURY TOURS

A TYPICAL gloomy November morning. Drizzle descends through the air. Rolf sets out from his latest temporary dwelling. He tramples through the damp piles of brown leaves strewn across the streets. The fog that briefly threatened to disrupt the international football match a couple of weeks earlier still hung around in pockets. The grim, lingering autumnal weather allied with the smell of decay from rotting leaves suited the mood of the British nation. Its people would mark Armistice Day, Friday, 11 November 1938; the anniversary of the end of the Great War. Hopes of avoiding another war slowly but surely seemed to be disappearing.

Rolf stopped outside a newsagent's shop. A rack of newspapers hung above billboards proclaiming the usual litany of awful news. One triggered an alarm. It gave him flashbacks to his home city and the Nazi-inspired hordes of thugs. The fear of them spiralling out of control. The message was simple, 'NAZIS ADMIT RIOTS – *Daily Mirror*.' Another, 'POGROM GOES ON TILL NIGHT – *Daily Express*' and 'GERMANY'S NIGHT OF TERROR – *Daily Herald*.'

It had taken 48 hours for news of the full extent of the horror of events in Germany to reach Britain. Rolf's visa secured by Bert Sproston was for a fortnight's stay in the UK from the date of the game between England and a European XI. As already noted, it was due to expire, on or about the fateful date of Wednesday, 9 November 1938. That date went down in history as *Kristallnacht* or, in English, 'the night of broken glass'. Rolf Friedland understandably wanted to stay in England, rather than be deported back to Nazi Germany.

Thugs targeted thousands of Jewish-owned businesses in Berlin and burned synagogues to the ground. Jewish-owned shops were looted. Of the 11 synagogues in Rolf's home city, nine were left as smouldering ruins. Foreign correspondents in Berlin described the German capital as looking as if it had been bombed. The Gestapo then began rounding up thousands of Jews in cities across Germany and Austria.

The Nazi leadership falsely claimed that the anti-Jewish riots were spontaneous. They cited the pretext for the carnage as the murder of a young German diplomat in Paris, Ernst vom Rath. He was killed by a teenage German refugee, Herschel Grynspan. His target had been the German ambassador, but he killed Vom Rath instead. Ironically, historians contend that the young diplomat was being watched by the Gestapo because of his own anti-Nazi sentiments. Far from being a single spontaneous night of violence, the anti-Semitic *Kristallnacht* terror campaign lasted for more than a week. Only the economic damage, with German city centres trashed, persuaded the Nazi leadership to call off their thugs' attack.

As he stood outside the newsagent's on a gloomy autumn morning, Rolf's eyes were drawn to the front-page photograph of the *Daily Express*. Nobody wanted war, except the Nazis. The traumas of the Great War still lived fresh in the collective memory and psyche of the British people. Disabled veterans lived among them. Surely there would be no repeat of such horrors? Nobody mad enough to begin a war? Rolf knew the tragic answer.

Almost mournfully, he picked up a copy of the 1938 Armistice Day edition of the *Express*. It showed a Berlin synagogue set alight by rioters, the roof in a state of collapse as flames engulfed the building. The Nazis pretended they were not responsible.

The *Daily Express* among other British newspapers had gone along with the Nazis' pretence. The orgy of violence had been spontaneous. Ordinary German folk had been provoked, the *Express* declared. Its front-page splash claimed that the rioters had defied propaganda minister, Joseph Goebbels. How could they? Goebbels broadcast for calm. It was a cynical move meant more for the benefit of international diplomacy than the German public. Anybody daft enough to believe the lies.

'The just and understandable wrath of the German people concerning the cowardly Jewish assassination of a German diplomat in Paris has blown off a lot of its steam during the night,' Goebbels began. 'In many towns and districts of the Reich, reprisals were taken on Jewish buildings and businesses. The urgent request is now given to the whole nation to discontinue at once any further demonstration against the Jews.' Ominously, Goebbels commented that the final answer to Jewry will come in the form of laws and decrees.

Advocates of appeasement took Goebbels's word seriously, at least the claim of spontaneous rioting. Rolf did not. Where are the protests against the violent destruction of his people? There were none. One conclusion dawned on opponents of the Nazi regime as synagogues burned to the ground on *Kristallnacht*. As war loomed in Europe, the Nazis enjoyed the support of most German people.

Rolf instinctively knew that the Nazis would have ordered the pogrom – more than just a guess. He needed no confirmation. Too much pain, too much suffering and hardship for him throughout the preceding years at the hands of Hitler's followers. All of it countered by a growing resolve to escape, even to board a train for the seeming mundanity of watching a football match rather than the true intent of making an asylum claim.

'All over Germany tonight the Jews are cowering in terror,' declared the Berlin correspondent of the *Daily Express*. 'Their shops are wrecked and looted, their synagogues are burning, their homes are at the mercy of gangs drunk with destruction.' Any accounts of protests against the destruction, he wondered, while flicking through the pages. The answer was no. It might just be poor journalism. More alarmingly there were none. The German public in general signalled to the Nazis their quiet approval.

Amid the violent orgy, the Nazis insisted that Jewish theatre, concert, cinema and similar performances were prohibited. They declared that in the past, these belonged in the hands of what was termed the 'Jewish cultural league'. Jewish newspapers and Jewish schools remained closed. Jewish kids were banned from other schools. Teachers in Nuremberg went as far as teaching only the New Testament in Bible classes. The Nazis banned references to Jews as the 'chosen race'.

Germany's Jewish population were the clear victims. In the initial stages of *Kristallnacht*, about 8,000 Jews were arrested in Rolf's home city of Berlin alone. None of their attackers. An estimated 25,000 Jews were arrested throughout Germany and Austria. The Nazis also accelerated their programme of wholescale confiscation of Jewish property and capital. They did so while openly admitting that Jews were being sent to the concentration camps of Buchenwald, Sachsenhausen and Dachau. They were yet to turn them into death camps.

Eva Gusdorf, the future Mrs Freeman, referred to *'Die Nacht der langer Messer,* (the night of the long knives) so prettily called these days, *Kristallnacht* (crystal night).' Eva preferred to quietly ignore Nazi thugs murdering each other earlier in the decade. On *Kristallnacht*, she witnessed what she called, 'The horror, the burning of synagogues, the arrest of innocent people, the burning of books, of shops, the destruction and the looting.' In the afternoon, her father was warned to leave Berlin. She remained in Berlin. Her father travelled to the Netherlands where she thought he was safe but he was not. Trapped in Amsterdam after Germany occupied the Netherlands, the Nazis captured him. The Red Cross informed Eva that her father, Hermann, had died in a concentration camp. Murdered to be precise.

Eva escaped from Berlin to Amsterdam on a 'tear filled' train, assisted by a Scandinavian diplomat who took pity on her. No need to involve an English professional footballer. Just before war broke out, she made it by ferry to the relative safety of London. 'Relative safety' because of the Blitz, then the V1 and V2 campaigns. As the 'doodle bugs' dropped on the British capital, Eva heard of her father's tragic fate.

In November 1938, British newspapers sympathetic to appeasement appeared, at first, to play down the severity of the attacks on Germany's Jewish population. Yet, there were clues in the days and hours leading up to *Kristallnacht*. On the morning of 9 November 1938, the *Daily Express* carried an account of the latest rambling speech from Hitler. It was the anniversary of the failed Nazi putsch in Munich of 1923. Hitler set out his determination to 'ensure the safety of the Reich to the limit'. War was about to be enacted against Germany. It was classic fascist paranoia and subterfuge. Hitler was planning to wage war, not his critics abroad. Rival nations, notably the UK, were ill-prepared in any case.

One man in particular just happened to be his target, the future British prime minister, Winston Churchill. Hitler declared, 'In England and France there are men at the helm who desire peace but there are others who want war against us, and it is that that I have to take into account, because according to their constitution, Mr Churchill could become prime minister of Britain tomorrow.'

Hitler's rant demonstrated that he clearly feared Churchill. He chillingly concluded, 'Taking it all in all, I am not a sovereign in the usual sense of the word. I am only the leader of the German people. I could have assumed quite different titles; you know that, my friends. I have renounced that privilege. I choose to remain what I have always been, and in that sense, Mr Churchill is an English deputy and I am the deputy of Germany, with the only difference perhaps, that Churchill only commands a small fraction of the votes whereas I command all the votes of Germany.'

Just to add pressure on British opponents of appeasement, Goebbels's newspaper *Angriff* ran a front-page story claiming that it had exposed 'Jewish murderers and their agitators'. Leading lights in this alleged conspiracy? 'It is no coincidence that while in London the Churchill clique were unmasked by Herr Hitler the murder weapon went off in the hand of a Jewish youth in Paris.' *Kristallnacht* began within hours.

Any foreign criticism following *Kristallnacht* was met by the Nazi-controlled press with further personal attacks aimed at British statesmen, Churchill the prime target. Even Neville Chamberlain appeared sympathetic to his political rival. Downing Street briefed the British press that the prime minister was shocked by both the violence and the subsequent outpouring of hatred towards Germany's critics. Any lingering hopes of Britain maintaining a policy of appeasement were shattered by *Kristallnacht*.

Safely ensconced in London, Rolf escaped the murderous orgy. There was zero chance of him going back to Berlin. Hundreds of his fearful compatriots, facing yet more draconian Nazi decrees targeting Jews, gathered outside the British and American embassies in Berlin hoping to secure a precious visa, a permit to leave Nazi Germany. Rolf won his freedom, effectively courtesy of a football ticket. Yet as these horrific accounts of the violence reached Britain, our young football refugee faced the possibility of deportation back to Germany.

For any jobsworth in the Home Office, he had technically outstayed his welcome. Jewish refugees had ended up in British courts to face deportation. For all the British condemnation of the Nazis, Jews in Britain still encountered anti-Semitic hostility. Immigrants, asylum seekers fleeing Nazi persecution, were not necessarily welcome. Not everyone was as open-minded as Bert Sproston.

His father's presence in London ought to have been an advantage. Instead, it perversely made life more difficult in trying to claim asylum, hence the unusual sleeping arrangements at White Hart Lane. His father told Rolf that his presence in England would negatively impact his own application. He was wrong. As much as Rolf endured a challenging relationship with his parents in childhood, he later cemented a loving bond with his father.

Rolf's next immediate challenge just happened to be overcoming anti-Semitism in what he hoped to be his adopted country. For outright hostility, the *Daily Mail* obliged. A *Mail* editorial commenting on *Kristallnacht* infamously claimed that while the attacks were an outrage, 'the treatment of German Jews by Germany is an internal affair'. Britain was not to even object, let alone interfere. Lord Rothermere's newspaper did not entirely welcome German-Jewish refugees coming to the United Kingdom.

Kristallnacht coincided, deliberately or otherwise, with the British government's Woodhead Commission into proposals to partition Palestine. Both Arabs and Jews rejected its findings. As Jewish buildings smouldered on the ground in Berlin, the *News Chronicle* newspaper in London led its front page with 'Palestine plan does not satisfy Arabs or Jews'.

Naturally, the Nazis played their part in helping to stir up anti-Semitism in other countries. The most striking observation was made by Hannah Arendt, a Jewish academic briefly imprisoned by the Gestapo, before fleeing to France and eventually the United States. She wrote in *The Origins of Totalitarianism*, 'The pre-war "solution" of the Jewish question was the outstanding export commodity of Nazi Germany: expulsion of Jews carried an important portion of Nazism into other countries; by forcing Jews to leave the Reich passportless and penniless, the legend of the Wandering Jew was realised.'

Arendt also noted that official SS newspaper *Das Schwarze Korps* stated in 1938 that if the world was not yet convinced that Jews were, in its words, 'the scum of the earth', it would be when 'identifiable beggars, without nationality, without money, and without passports crossed their frontiers'. Quite brazenly, the Nazis used the reluctance of some states to welcome Jewish refugees as proof that no such thing as human rights existed. Those idealists advocating human rights just happened, in the Nazi view, to be men and women of feeble-minded hypocrisy.

Against this depressing backdrop, Rolf sought help from London's Jewish community. Life in London was relatively comfortable for him, even his brief time sleeping on Tottenham's dressing-room benches. Bert Sproston was not alone in assisting him. Among the notes Rolf carefully hid away in his suitcase, he had details of those who might help him in London. These were given to him by highly organised Jewish refugee groups still operating in the German capital. He found somewhere to live at a refuge in Fitzrovia, just close to London's central synagogue.

Relying on a professional footballer's kindness was never going to be enough. Perusing British newspapers with accounts of *Kristallnacht* and just shrugging his shoulders never worked either. He needed to do more, both to secure his future in England and use his new-found freedom to combat the ideology of intolerance.

Rolf received word from his new friends of protests to be held against the pogroms outside the Germany embassy at Carlton Terrace, just off Regent Street in London. The protestors were to gather in Hyde Park.

Before setting off for the gathering, Rolf quickly checked the football results. He needed, out of habit, to be in touch with the most human of priorities for any sports fan. Always read the back pages of a newspaper first. A sports fan would understand, nobody else. He already knew that his adopted club Spurs had drawn 2-2 with Bradford Park Avenue at White Hart Lane. He was at the game. As for his mate Bert Sproston? He had mysteriously left Tottenham Hotspur. Quite why puzzled Rolf as much as any Spurs fan.

Bert played for Manchester City in a 2-1 win away at Southampton. Rolf was unconcerned that he went off injured. 'Why did Bert leave Spurs?' Rolf wondered. 'Why go to just another second division club, albeit recent league champions?' Rolf noted from the Sunday newspapers that Derby County were still the first division league leaders. They lost to Charlton Athletic – a club perhaps to visit just on the other side of the River Thames. Football gave him an early guide to Britain's geography.

He grabbed his coat and headed for Hyde Park. A chance to protest against the evil of Nazism, to demonstrate solidarity with other refugees fleeing tyranny. A chance also to meet new friends, renew old friendships. Candle-lit synagogues, especially around Whitechapel in London, held prayers throughout the weekend. Young Jewish men and women joined a different vigil. As they paraded in wind and rain from Hyde Park, banners were held aloft. 'Protest against Nazi terrorism', declared one. 'A thousand years of persecution' asserted another. All chanted as they marched before being met by a phalanx of police on Lower Regent Street.

The protestors stood a few hundred yards from the embassy as the rain poured down. It was no hardship for Rolf and his new friends. A couple of them were allowed through the police cordon to take a letter of protest to the German embassy. It was an important but rather pointless gesture. Newspapers claimed that the protesters eventually dispersed, many of them looking subdued.

What to expect? A riot? Rolf was possibly too young to remember the Berlin police, Nazis and communists in violent clashes during the Weimar Republic. Many of his new friends did remember London's Battle of Cable Street as it slowly entered political folklore. On 4 October police tried to escort around 3,000 fascist marchers through the East End, specifically Whitechapel – an area with London's largest Jewish population. They failed. An estimated crowd of 50,000 anti-fascists, Jewish residents and Irish immigrants along with trade unionists, stopped them. Dozens of people were injured in the violent clashes.

The then home secretary, Sir John Simon, decided to act against the far right. Sir John, who as a reminder privately expressed concerns over the arrival of Nazi German football fans in London, pushed the Public Order Act of 1936 through parliament. It banned the wearing of uniforms by political groups. It also banned quasi-military organisations, any group 'trained or equipped for the purpose of enabling them to be employed in usurping the functions of the police or of the armed forces of the Crown". These measures remain as Westminster statute law to this day. It is against the law for any political grouping to act as a conventional fascist party, one replete with uniforms.

Unlike in Germany, Italy or Spain, fascism struggled as a political doctrine to take firm root in Britain. Rolf, as he joined the march protesting against *Kristallnacht* in November 1938, knew first hand of the dangers of fascism. Nazi totalitarian rule, racism and the desire to spread their evil creed as a cancer throughout Europe. There was an important battle to come, a war. He was grateful to those kind enough to offer him sanctuary in England, a democratic and largely tolerant country. Above all, he was grateful to a footballer with itchy feet.

As London began to crank back into life on the following morning, Rolf went back to the offices of the German-Jewish Aid Council at Woburn House on Upper Woburn Place in Bloomsbury. It was also the office of the chief rabbi. The staff managed to extend his visa and then set him up with a job at a market garden near Chesham in Buckinghamshire.

They did remarkable refugee work, agriculture becoming a key sector for them to find young male refugees work. Otto Schiff, the chairman of the German-Jewish Aid Committee, revealed that its staff of 250 at Woburn House received 4,000 letters and between 600 and 800 calls per day. His operation cost between £5,000 and £7,000 a week (roughly £200,000 to £300,000 a week in today's money).

The work intensified in the aftermath of *Kristallnacht*. Schiff led the campaign for donations to help refugees. He toured synagogues throughout the UK stressing that his Jewish friends were fortunate to live in a land where the ideals of democracy were treasured. In facing the Nazis before even a shot was fired in war, democracy was fighting for freedom and decency. Otto Schiff inspired many, Rolf included.

Once settling into English life, he appreciated the charitable spirit of those around him. Rather than dwell on your own problems, help those less fortunate than yourself. Actually, forget political campaigners raising funds such as Mr Schiff. An England footballer served as a bigger mentor to Rolf, a greater and unlikelier inspiration. Rolf recognised Bert's humanity in his compatriots, even many of his fellow footballers.

As a big-city boy, born and brought up in Berlin, Rolf was happy with life in London. He was just as happy to move out to rural Hertfordshire. His work allowed him for a brief while to save enough cash for a fortnightly ritual. Board a train, one free of guards in their sinister uniform, wait for the whistle to go as doors slammed shut, set off for White Hart Lane station, and go to watch Tottenham Hotspur.

Football allowed working men of all ages a break from everyday life. Unfortunately, as already mentioned, his favourite player, Bert Sproston, no longer played for Tottenham Hotspur. He was less happy with life in London. How to settle a bout of homesickness? His mum's lovingly home-cooked steak and kidney pudding.

A HOMESICK FOOTBALLER

BONFIRE NIGHT loomed and Bert was about to join the fireworks, about to explode. 'Just why is my form fizzling out?' he frustratingly wondered. There was just no sign of him exploding into life on the football field. Sporting success needs a sound mind as well as a sound body. Sadly, life in the big city never suited him. He wanted to leave; the only way to escape his bizarre mental torture.

Even the greatest footballers suffer dips in form. Bert, as a down-to-earth figure, knew he was good enough to play international football but he was hardly the greatest. His mate Stanley Matthews enjoyed such an accolade. How to recover form, he wondered. The answer was easy – find another club. He told himself, 'Go back north, young man.'

Fans stood on the terraces mystified by his drop in form. More importantly, so too did his manager. Ted McWilliams spent a large sum of money on the England defender, at least a large sum for the era. McWilliams looked on despairingly at his international full-back's performances. The disappointing showings were evident during his player's exposure on the national stage with the England team.

How does a football manager deal with disaffected players? Quite simple – most get rid of them, or to be more polite, allow them to leave. Bert returned from international duty intent on a meeting with his manager as he wanted to put in a transfer request. It would not come as a surprise if it was rejected. After all, he had only been at the club four months. Leeds United had transferred him for a record sum.

Once Bert knocked on the door, McWilliams welcomed him in. Much to the player's surprise his manager appeared fairly relaxed. 'Fine Bert, you can leave.' It was clear the player was unhappy with London life. There was just the important matter of finding a suitable club, one willing to stump up the cash McWilliams paid for Sproston during the summer.

After Rolf Friedland's brief sojourn in the Tottenham Hotspur dressing rooms, he became a fan of the club for life. Bert Sproston was less keen on Spurs and London in general. McWilliams knew it was pointless trying to keep him. Bert returned to his family home at Sandbach in Cheshire and waited for the call from Manchester City.

McWilliams began talks over the transfer of Sproston with a slightly surprised Manchester City manager, Wilf Wild, at the game between the English and Scottish leagues at Molineux on Wednesday, 2 November 1938. The host club, Wolves, were not interested in signing Sproston. As for the game itself, the Football League beat the Scottish League 3-1 to claim the inter-league title. It was a dubious honour for English football as the Scots had sent a weakened team to Wolverhampton.

The following morning, Wild and his vice-chairman, Albert Alexander, went to London to finalise the talks. Up until then, Sproston was the only player signed by Spurs for what was thought to be a five-figure sum. It was supposed to herald a new era of Spurs being a 'big buying' club but that turned out to be an idle boast. Manchester City, another second division club despite winning the league title only 15 months earlier, agreed to stump up £10,000 for Sproston – the same amount Tottenham Hotspur paid to Leeds United.

Spurs fielded their international full-back from Leeds for just nine matches. Sproston was more than willing to leave. His transfer to Manchester City came as a relief. It was the best on offer. 'I know it is a shock,' the Spurs secretary, Arthur Turner, commented. 'Nobody is more disappointed than Sproston himself at his inability to get acclimatised to London. He tried hard and the club did everything that was possible, but it would not work out. We concluded, finally, that Sproston would never be comfortable away from the north – and there you are.'

By the time the clubs agreed to the transfer, Bert sat patiently with his mother in her living room. They waited for the call for him to go to Maine Road. Tottenham Hotspur quite unusually gave him permission to spend the week in Sandbach. He was not training with the rest of the Spurs squad. His brief time as a Spurs player was over.

Nothing would be agreed without the approval of Alice Sproston. For the second time in four months, the telegram boy arrived at the door with instructions for Bert to sign for another club. Before going to Maine Road, he waited for a copy of the contract to be sent to his mother. Bert only signed the transfer forms on Friday, 4 November 1938, once agreed and overseen by Alice. Tottenham Hotspur insisted the sum involved was the same they paid to Leeds United, not a penny more, not a penny less.

Curiously enough and by pure coincidence, he made his debut for Manchester City the following day against Tottenham Hotspur at Maine Road. The City programme listed Bert Sproston as the club's opposing right-back. Instead, he donned a sky-blue shirt for the first time. More than 46,000 fans turned up at Maine Road, the biggest crowd of the season so far, and City won 2-0. Scribbling in changes to programme line-ups turned out to be a matter of curious joviality for puzzled fans.

The *Daily Express* thought the Manchester City crowd all felt a little cross-eyed, mystified by the man named on the Spurs teamsheet playing for their club instead. It had helpfully offered them clues on its Saturday morning front page. Bert Sproston wanted to move from Tottenham to Manchester City because his mum lived in nearby Sandbach, he loved her steak and kidney pudding, and because he was unable to play well enough while living so far away from his childhood home. Hence, the surprise transfer.

At the final whistle, Sproston's old Spurs team-mates graciously singled him out for congratulations. Just perhaps, it more than likely rankled with them that Bert had recovered his old form. If so, it failed to prevent any display of sportsmanship. He was still their mate and an international player to be respected.

Clifford Webb of the *Daily Herald* noted on the morning of the game, 'Frankly, I have felt that Sproston's form this season has not been so good as it was during the 1937/38 campaign, when he first attracted the attention of the [England] selectors.' He was not alone in such a view. John Robertson of the *Sunday Mirror* moaned, 'Sproston was congratulated by his old Spurs colleagues, but I still feel that he should not have been transferred until this match was over. Unwittingly, Spurs have given supporters the impression that sentiment has no place in their make-up and that money is the be-all and end-all of football.' Football fans in the Premier League era almost a century later might be familiar with the sentiment.

Before the game Sproston reflected on his shock move back up north. 'People may think I am a bit dopey, but I love my home and the country around here,' he told reporters at his Sandbach home. 'I am just about fed up with "digs". With all the good will in the world people cannot look after you like they do at home. I had a good home in Leeds, but even then, I was happier when I was able to come home between matches.

'I made a big mistake in moving south. London is all right for a man with no home ties. But it didn't suit me well, and I am very sorry to have upset their side, but when you feel you are out of your element what can you do? Home surroundings and plain good food were the things that I needed most. Now I have them I think I shall do well.' His favourite plain good food? It was unquestionably his mother's steak and kidney pudding.

Spurs gave their reasons to fans for selling Sproston in the programme notes for a game against their old friends from Bradford Park Avenue on 12 November 1938: 'Would it have been fair to Sproston, and would it have been in the interests of the Spurs to have insisted upon the maintenance of his active connection with us? The directors and Mr McWilliams [manager Ted] reluctantly came to the conclusion that the question must be answered in the negative. Sproston, who is a delightful fellow, leaves the Spurs with the most sincere wishes of all for his future success on the field.'

McWilliams commented, 'It was absolutely impossible to keep him. He would have become really ill if he stayed here. The transfer was in the best interests of the player and the club, but it was a tragedy for us to lose such a great player. We would very much rather have the player than the money.' As for signing a replacement? 'There are not many Sprostons knocking about,' concluded McWilliams. His concern for his players' mental health was noteworthy. The Spurs manager was ahead of his time.

It was perhaps for the best that Bert would never have picked up a copy of London's *Evening News* outside the capital. Spurs fans were less sanguine about his departure than the club's board and its manager. J. G. Orange claimed he met fans vowing never to return to White Hart Lane, such was their anger at Sproston's departure, commenting, 'I cannot understand how a man, after playing only nine games for a club that paid £8,000 for his transfer, arrived at a decision that the place did not suit his health. Nor can I understand why Tottenham Hotspur, who are so much in need of good footballers, should let him go so easily. Whether there was anything further in the case than this matter of health I do not profess to know, but the public seem to have it in their minds that there was. I don't know whether Sproston expected to find a job in London to swell his football wages, but whatever the cause of his dissatisfaction with this part of the world, he did not give himself a very long time to acclimatise his football or his health to it.'

The irate correspondent speculated that fortunately for London other players, maybe better players, might take the risk of playing for London clubs. There was nothing more for Bert to do than ignore the criticism and renew his career at Manchester City. He had been selected to play for England against Norway as a Tottenham Hotspur player. He turned out for his country as a Manchester City player. The team was selected after the inter-league game at Molineux, at which his transfer was agreed. The game against Norway turned out to be his last appearance for England, barring a couple of wartime internationals. The game also took place on the significant date of 9 November 1938 – *Kristallnacht*.

Fans turning up at St James' Park in Newcastle enjoyed what many in the crowd considered to be an exhibition game rather than an international. England won 4-0. One of the delighted selectors went into the England dressing room at half-time urging the team to score more goals. They were 4-0 up at the interval. The second half was goalless, despite the odd foray in attack by the England right-back.

Sproston left the field happy with his performance. Along with Hapgood and Cullis, Henry Rose singled him out as 'brilliant' in defence. Charles Buchan agreed, writing in the *News Chronicle*, 'Sproston reached his best form before he became over-confident and nearly gave away two goals by trying to dribble around his opponents near his own goal.' Why not give it a try, thought Sproston? He regained his famous powers of recovery as well as his old form. Football was meant to be fun and Bert was more than happy to demonstrate that. The Norwegian forwards failed to take advantage of any slips. His place as an England international no longer seemed under threat.

After the game, the selectors met and kept Sproston in the side to play Ireland at Old Trafford. Bert looked forward to a match just up the road from his family home in Sandbach. Unfortunately, he picked up an injury in City's next league game on 12 November 1938 against Southampton. Until then, Sproston appeared to be regaining the impressive form he once showed at Leeds. City beat Saints 2-1. The Press Association reporter commented, 'Sproston's calm judgement pulled them through many awkward situations.' But after the referee blew the final whistle, Sproston hobbled off the field. He pulled out of England's game against Ireland a few days later, suffering from a niggle. Little did Bert know, but it was effectively the end of his international career.

Bert waited at his home in Sandbach, hoping for an international recall. It never came. His return to fitness and to White Hart Lane on 11 March 1939 provided an ideal opportunity to impress the selectors. His performance certainly impressed Spurs fans, at least until the final minute. Sproston left the field for ten minutes in the first half, nursing a thigh injury. Once his leg was strapped up, he returned to the field. The use of substitutes was still almost three decades off in English football. Sproston went out on the left wing, theoretically, in the view of the *Manchester Evening News,* a lame-duck player. It then hailed him as the 'hero of a great Manchester City fight'. Apparently, City's emergency winger was 'terrific'.

He gave his side the lead on the 65th minute, latching on to a loose ball despite visibly limping, and thumping the ball into the net. Spurs equalised to make the score 2-2. But with just three minutes to go, Sproston scored the winner. 'They've forgotten about me,' Bert must have thought as he stood unmarked by the edge of the left-hand post. Maurice Dunkley then sent in a perfect cross. Standing effectively on one leg, Bert leapt just slightly for a neat header into the goal. Manchester City won 3-2. The results ended Spurs' hopes of promotion. Afterwards, he told the Spurs players that he would rather have scored his two goals against any other opposition. As for his last-minute winner, 'I really didn't want to do it, but I just had to.'

The north London newspaper, the *Weekly Herald,* was not best pleased. Before the game, its columnist Spectator mocked Sproston's excuse for leaving north London. 'He left London because he was homesick, and he was badly advised when he allowed a suet firm to advertise that he went home because he wanted his mother's puddings made with that firm's suet!'

The following week a chastened Spectator informed *Weekly Herald* readers, 'Truth is stranger than fiction. If you had read in a story book of what actually took place at Tottenham on Saturday you would have said, "Ah, but them things only happen in books." Unfortunately for the Spurs, the happenings on Saturday were real and they virtually extinguished hopes of winning promotion this season. The fairy story feature of the match was that Bert Sproston, who was playing against his old club, scored two of Manchester City's three goals despite the fact that he was playing at outside-left as a cripple.' The fairy tale had a twist.

His encouraging form and goalscoring exploits were never enough for an England recall. Certainly not while carrying yet another injury. After losing to Scotland at Wembley in April 1938, Bert looked forward, in his mind, to putting the record straight. Vengeance over the auld enemy at Hampden Park. The chance never came, not even in forthcoming wartime internationals.

Bert was resigned to his fate. Injury at White Hart Lane came as a deeply frustrating setback. At home he picked up the *Evening Sentinel* for Monday, 27 March 1939. The Stoke-on-Trent-based newspaper naturally highlighted that Stoke City's Stanley Matthews had kept his place for the game against Scotland. Well done, Stan. Sadly, there was no place for Sandbach boy Bert Sproston as injury had ruled him out. To make matters worse, he was not needed for the planned post-season tour of Europe, including a game against world champions Italy at the San Siro in Milan. Once an automatic choice for England, Sproston suffered rejection.

Intriguingly, the *Sentinel* also ran a story of 15 German footballers calling off their visit to the Potteries. They were from the four clubs Stoke City were due to play on a post-season tour of Germany. The DFB regretted it felt the need to take the decision. Stoke City revealed that unless 'adverse circumstances arise' in international relations then its players would indeed still go to Germany for games in Hamburg, Berlin, Düsseldorf and Nuremberg. Harold Booth, the club's chairman, revealed that it made the decision after taking 'advice'. He did not reveal the source of this advice, whether it was from the FA or Foreign Office. On 3 April 1939, his board changed their minds and called off the tour of Germany.

For all his disappointment as a footballer, Bert realised he might avoid more personal embarrassment. There was to be no act of folly to explain away to his friend Rolf, let alone his own family. Facing Italy once again provided England's players with another unwelcome diplomatic challenge. They dutifully met it. They gave their dubious example of courtesy to fascist opponents before the opening match of their European tour of 1939 at the San Siro.

In pure footballing terms, the game against Italy made sense. As world champions, the Italians wanted to show the English just how much they had matured. Italian fans, or at least their newspapers, referred to the English as the 'fathers of football' rather than the 'masters of football'. England's footballers travelled to Milan admitting to a touch of trepidation. Unfortunately, there was to be a repeat of a fascist salute by England's footballers. As much as Bert was unhappy to be left out of the team, he avoided another order to indulge in another act of shame. The game itself ended in a 2-2 draw.

As war became more inevitable by the day, football seemed like a distraction, even for hardened professionals such as Bert Sproston. It did take the minds off supporters and players alike of the feeling of gloom engulfing the nation. Football, more than ever, provided brief escapism.

Bert knew all too well from his fateful visit to Germany of the dangers posed by the Nazis. He gave the Hitler salute in Berlin along with his team-mates as part of a futile attempt to avoid war. Once he met Rolf after the game, his conscience prompted him to reflect on the awful nature of the Nazi threat. He already knew that Hitler was an 'evil little twat'. Rolf's plight, his desperate pleas for salvation, confirmed Bert's worst fears. Hence, he persuaded the FA to help rescue the football-crazy Jewish teenager from Germany.

The 1939/40 season began with fans and players alike resigned to the possibility that it would never be finished. Football mattered less and less to the British public and Bert noticed the large gaps on the terraces as he lined up for Manchester City at Maine Road. On 2 September 1939, City beat Chesterfield 2-0 in the old second division. A disappointing crowd of 18,000 turned up to watch the game. Attendances slumped that weekend from the early season average across the Football League. Hitler had ordered the invasion of Poland the day before Bert ran out to face the Spireites. No prayers to the heavens prevented war, and certainly not the British government's hapless appeasement policies. Nazi forces crossed the border into Poland on Friday, 1 September 1939. The following Sunday was even quieter than usual, aside from the millions filing into church. Even those lapsed from their faith offered prayers. Once religious observance was over, the nation tuned into the BBC.

Bert supped a cup of tea as he sat by the wireless set in his parents' living room. His mum had just put on the family's Sunday lunch in the kitchen. She sat down beside his dad. His brothers nervously slipped through the door. No football training today in the Sproston household. More than 100 miles away in rural

Hertfordshire, Rolf gathered with his workmates outside the open window of a farmhouse. Their boss turned up the BBC Home Service to full volume. It was 3 September 1939. The entire British nation held its breath.

After Hitler's troops invaded Poland, the British government set an ultimatum for Nazi forces to withdraw. Just after 11am, the British prime minister, Neville Chamberlain, came on the radio to announce, 'I am speaking to you from the Cabinet Room of 10 Downing Street. This morning the British ambassador in Berlin handed the German government a final note, stating that unless we heard from them – by 11 o'clock – that they were prepared at once to withdraw their troops from Poland, a state of war would exist between us. I have to tell you now that no such undertaking has been received and that, consequently, this country is at war with Germany.'

Bert made his decision. 'I need to sign up.' Within weeks he joined the British Army as a physical training instructor. Sergeant Sproston was assigned to the Tank Corps. Professional footballers were in demand. Hundreds had already signed up as reservists.

As for Rolf? It was a little more difficult for a German to sign up to fight Germans. The armed forces took their time in welcoming German-speaking Jews into the British ranks. But why shy away from a challenge? Certainly, there was no chance of the football refugee from the Nazis doing so.

BERT'S WAR

NOTHING MORE trivial than sport? Bert argued otherwise. Sport mattered to him, not just because he earned a living from playing football, but it was conducive to boosting physical and mental wellbeing. The football industry had its faults but he also recognised that it was a privilege to be paid to play football, a sport he loved.

The teenage boy he helped to rescue from Berlin shared Bert's love of the beautiful game. As a teenager, he was quite mercenary in picking up spare cash but it was only a game. As for the benefits from maintaining physical fitness, he was no fan of Hitler's concept of *Wehrsport* – sport as preparation for war. Sport was important to him. It was also meant to be fun.

Once Britain declared war on Germany, all games ended abruptly. Not least the diplomatic and political games that ended up bringing shame to the Nazi-saluting England football team. Children's ball games played by adults for money also ended. Chamberlain's government decreed that there was no room for fun in wartime Britain. As Britain went to war, the government cancelled all spectator sports, at least for the time being. A trip to the cinema or theatre? Forget it.

As the dull but measured tones of Neville Chamberlain declaring war on Germany cascaded from the radio, Rolf felt curiously inspired. A surge of idealism emboldened him. He had idealistic reasons for trying to join the British Army. After all, he was a German Jewish refugee, who escaped the Nazis. Rolf had witnessed the descent into depravity during his formative years. Now, he wanted to confront the evil.

For Bert, he had a less idealistic reason to join the army – he needed a job. No professional football, so, no job. Working with his brothers in their Sandbach building firm was an option to fall back on but he dismissed such an idea. He had shares in the firm but had given them up. Of course, he was also more than aware of the evil nature of the Nazi threat. He had met them, witnessed the fanaticism. They needed to be confronted. So, it was the army life for him.

Both young men, along with the rest of Britain, expected the bombs to fall soon, the artillery anti-aircraft batteries to open up and the potential terror of gas attacks. Britain was at war. But in the autumn of 1939, a phoney war began. Nothing phoney in the legions of children they both saw disembarking from trains in rural England, gas masks and name tags hung around their necks. They stood on railway platforms confused, disoriented and understandably frightened.

Rolf understood the reasons for boarding a train to safety. He had effectively done the same by boarding a train from Berlin Zoologischer Garten station on the grounds of going to watch an international football match. He was off to the sanctuary and safety of a new life in Britain. For worried parents waving off their children, they were temporarily sending them off for a new life. Britain's major cities were no longer safe. Additionally, as an almost trivial matter, football no longer provided a welcome relief from the pains of everyday life.

Bert suddenly found a cure for his homesickness. No longer employed by Manchester City, he patiently waited at Sandbach station for his train. Once again, he was heading south but not to the capital city. Life as a physical training instructor in the army town of Aldershot awaited.

On the day Chamberlain declared war on Germany, parliament introduced conscription. The National Service (Armed Forces) Act 1939 imposed conscription on all males living in Great Britain aged between 18 and 41 who had to register for service. Those medically unfit were exempted, as were others in key industries and jobs such as baking, farming, medicine and engineering. Professional footballers were not exempt.

Any chance of turning out anytime soon before the adoring masses of tens of thousands at Wembley or Hampden Park seemed remote. Competitive football watched by spectators while there was a war on? Bert was resigned to the answer being no.

But was it a little premature to call off football altogether? Surely football, any sport, might lift deflated spirits? Stanley Rous, the FA boss who encouraged Bert Sproston and the rest of the England team to make the Nazi salute in Berlin, recalled, 'We had no expectation that there would be such a leisurely start to hostilities for us, and all was bustle at first as the evacuees were hurried out of London and the volunteers and reservists hastened to join the forces. As Britain concentrated on war all regular sporting fixtures ended, and football momentarily seemed irrelevant.'

Before the war, Rous thought that he had come up with a cunning plan in the event of hostilities. His plan was worthy of Baldrick in the BBC comedy series, *Blackadder*. It was next to useless. The FA decreed after the tour of Germany, Switzerland and France in May 1938, 'That in the event of war, a meeting be convened comprising the officers of the Football Association and the management committee of the Football League for the purpose of deciding the course of action to be taken with regard to the game.'

Setting up a talking shop hardly helped Bert and hundreds of other full-time professional footballers. There were an estimated 3,000 players in the English and Scottish leagues. Sports correspondents pointed out that rugby league players were slightly more fortunate. Most of them were employed by their clubs on a part-time basis. They simply had the option of falling back on their jobs outside of rugby league to earn a living. Many of those jobs were reserved occupations.

At least that was the theory. Many footballers and rugby league players volunteered for the armed services. They did their 'bit' to use the language of the time. They were cleared to volunteer for the armed forces almost a fortnight before war was declared. Up until then, the FA banned soldiers, airmen and sailors from professional football. On 21 August 1939, the FA waived rule 33 which stated, 'No player serving in His Majesty's Armed Forces could be registered as a professional footballer.'

As alluded to earlier, Bert had thought of going back to work as a plumber, the trade he gave up for football. His brother, Jack, ran a successful building firm. No problem in finding a job there, even in wartime. The nation needed builders. Every Luftwaffe bombing raid would sadly make their work all the more urgent. Manchester City team-mate, Irish international Peter Doherty, worked for the Sprostons of Sandbach. The club insisted that he needed to remain within easy reach of Manchester despite not offering him any alternative source of employment. Doherty turned down work in Glasgow. He was grateful to find work with the Sproston family.

He eventually volunteered to join the RAF, occasionally playing football against Bert in inter-services matches.

Instead of joining the family firm, Bert volunteered almost immediately for military service in autumn 1939. He saw little point in waiting for a decision by the football authorities on whether to persevere with the professional game. Eventually, it was confirmed that there were to be no professional football contracts for the remainder of the war. Forget any notions of playing football being a reserved occupation. There were other more fruitful uses for players.

Army historian, Alf Coulton, commented, 'Professional football players, managers, coaches, trainers and masseurs were ideally suited to the pressing need of knocking a conscript army into sound physical shape, as required by the War Office.' Footballers quickly established themselves as the backbone of physical training in the armed forces. Those who were conscripted or enlisted into the army were sent to do their training and studying on fast-track courses at the Army School of Physical Training (ASPT) Aldershot, which was referred to in those days (by the footballers) as the 'Muscle Factory'.

Along with hundreds of others, Bert emerged as a sergeant instructor with the Army Physical Training Corps (APTC). Sgt Sproston was later seconded as a physical training instructor to the role in the Royal Artillery's Army Tank Corps. Arsenal's manager, George Allison, caught up with him in a piece for the national newspapers. He did so while announcing plans for Arsenal to play an army team at Aldershot just before Christmas, 1939.

'Young Sergeant Bert Sproston, of Leeds, Tottenham, and Manchester City fame, is, I believe, with the Tank Corps,' Allison wrote. 'Bert naively says, "I have nearly 600 men, two footballs and one rugby ball." Then, of course, follows an appeal for more equipment, which I know the Football Association will not leave unanswered. Bert's battalion, he says, is a very sporty one. It holds the Territorial Army (TA) Football Cup and has not lost a match for over a year. "They are expecting me to uphold that standard." You bet your life he will.'

As for fans such as Rolf, the absence of football or any sport to watch on Saturday afternoons was nothing more than a nuisance. But football was ingrained into 1930s British society. The working classes packed out stadiums. King George VI, a keen sportsman, professed to being a fan, albeit arguably rare among the rugby-obsessed ruling classes of the day. Association football provided a valuable and a powerful release from everyday life. In helping to escape the overbearing burdens of war, sport potentially provided a valuable service.

The FA, the Football League and, above all, the Chamberlain government were all a bit confused about the role of sport in society. Yes, it was a chance for the proverbial butcher, the baker and candlestick maker to make a bob or two on the side. Anything else? Not sure.

The mess left by constant sporting links to Germany in the spirit of appeasement gave a clue. The British government was indeed clueless about sport, specifically football. Its attempts to use it as a lame tool of diplomatic soft power turned out to be at best, misguided and at worst, embarrassingly futile. The Nazi salute by Sproston and company in Berlin served as an infamous demonstration.

In contrast, the Nazis clinically identified the role for sport in their strictly controlled society. It had a role of course in building physical fitness in young men going off to war, *Wehrsport* (military sport). But they also used sport for propaganda purposes, to promote the supposed superiority of the Aryan people. Making the German man or woman in the street feel better about themselves just happened to be a by-product. National triumphs on the sports field were to be celebrated. The Nazis eyed a greater triumph and did so in war.

Once Hitler's 1936 Olympics in Berlin were out of the way, the head of his SA, Victor Lutze told the Nazi newspaper *Völkischer Beobachter* that it was the task of sport to adapt itself to the new Germany. Lutz declared on 27 August 1937, 'In the Germany of the future sport will be only that which is of direct use to Germany – that which serves the ends of toughening the body and rendering it capable for military service. The fighting spirit, the mental spirit and bodily steeling [*körperliche Stählung*] of our men, will penetrate right through the philosophy of the Third Reich.' Lutze then commented, 'It is not important whether the leader of a company requires 10.8 seconds for a 100 metres race. What is important is whether he can bring 200 rifles into action as quickly as possible.'

Such a cynical view of sport barely occurred to British politicians, nor its value to the military. As Bert Sproston found potentially to his reputational cost in Berlin, British sportsmen were simply expected to be jolly good chaps while competing abroad. As a reminder, he was left baffled sat in a cafe as Stanley Matthews told him of plans to offer a Hitler salute as England players. Bafflement turned to anger as they grabbed their England shirts before going out to play Germany in Berlin's Olympiastadion. Both countries were off to war with each other. The British government's view of sport as being of national and diplomatic importance evolved. It did so slowly, very slowly – even in the post-war years.

Football League clubs pleaded with their players not to rush into any decision. Please do not pack your bags and head for the nearest army recruitment office. At least do not do so until after the FA and Football League clubs agreed on how to cope with the crisis. No matter that they had held earnest talks 12 months earlier into how to cope with the predictable outbreak of war. No, just wait for more deliberations from the committee men. Football clubs from Victorian times to modern times tend to specialise in farce.

The Football League president, William Cuff, declared, 'I do not think the clubs should allow their players to disperse.' Then he menacingly added, 'If a declaration of war makes it impossible for the terms of the contract to be fulfilled, the club owes no liability to the player and the player no liability to the club.' Clubs ruled the game, players were their glorified serfs.

Before, during and after the war, professional footballers harboured resentment. As Bert knew, none of the FA and Football League's prevarication over the staging of games amid the hostilities helped. It did not allow him to pay his keep at his parents' house in Sandbach. Nor did it help put food on the table for the young families of his colleagues.

One frustrated club manager told journalists on condition of anonymity, 'We are advised to ask our players to stand by. But how can we say that they should stand by when we also say that their contracts are cancelled and that they aren't entitled to payment? And how can clubs already mortgaged up to the neck pay wages without gates?'

In answering speculation that football might return to help boost morale, Cuff said, 'I am afraid the country can't have it both ways. If football is to come back and provide public entertainment it has got to have the entertainers, and I am afraid many of the boys will not be available if there isn't a settlement of this problems very soon.' Charles Buchan lamented, 'It is indeed a sad blow. I had half expected that the game would go on in some moderated form like it did in similar circumstances 25 years ago [the outbreak of the Great War]. The times are troublous enough without forbidding all forms of entertainment, especially those taking place in daylight hours, and I know of no better way of relieving the tension than by watching games like football.'

Buchan declared that the game was dead. But he hoped for a resurrection. 'I am not without hope that very soon the game will burst into life in a way that will not interfere with the bigger job on hand but will help it to some extent. After all there are men waiting to be called up, men engaged in important national work, men in key positions and, most important of all, soldiers themselves who are capable of and only too willing to divert the minds of the public, especially those engaged on munition work, from distressful affairs if only for a little while.'

Players were already leaving for the military or in some cases, especially in London, the police reserve. Football grounds were described as sombre, silent places, including the vast terraces at Manchester City's Maine Road. A few grounds had been commandeered by the military. Clifford Webb of the *Daily Herald* thought there were grounds for optimism. There would be a limited number of sporting diversions. 'The army boys with the time to spare ought to be able to provide some good football,' he speculated.

Bert Sproston was one of those army boys. But as Bert anticipated, he would spend much of the war out of the country. There was a world war on. Little did he anticipate but life as a physical training instructor in the army would ensure months on end spent at sea. A life on the ocean waves beckoned. He spent more than 21 months at sea, taking him to South Africa, India plus the battle zones of north Africa, Greece and Italy. Along with deployments to the European mainland as war came to an end, he was to visit all corners of a disintegrating British Empire.

In his time back on land in 'Blighty', he guested, in common with his fellow professionals, with clubs other than his own. Exiled back in the capital, the former England defender played mostly for Millwall, not in defence, but as a striker. Even as a youngster at Sandbach Ramblers, he was not so ambitious when it came to playing out of position. His most prolific season for Millwall was in 1942/43, making seven appearances and scoring six goals.

The ban on entertainment at cinemas, theatres and sports grounds had been lifted by the British government within a week of the declaration of war. The Sproston family would have approved of their evening newspaper's verdict. The *Evening Sentinel* commented, 'There is no frivolity about wartime sport. It keeps bodies and minds in good fettle and provides people with something to talk about besides war and the heavy round of service and work which is everybody's task.' The *Sentinel* had one answer to the question of how best to maintain morale, good spirits, and boosting confidence among the British people. It was, 'football, cinemas and theatres'.

Stanley Rous recalled in his 1978 autobiography *Football Worlds*, 'Before long we were also organising international friendlies as part of the endeavour to shrug off the discomforts of war, the bombing, the rationing, the restrictions on everyday life. Just because our lives were so cramped, and because the threat of sudden death was with civilians as well as soldiers, there was a heightened enjoyment, an uninhibited relish among players and spectators, which made these matches a special appearance.'

Settled into barracks at Aldershot, Bert Sproston laced up his boots for the first of the representative games of the war. An FA XI was due to play an army side of soldiers stationed at Aldershot on Saturday, 14 October 1939. Six of the army team, including Sproston, were internationals. Limitations were placed on the size of crowds allowed at football grounds to between 5,000 and 8,000. Aldershot FC rarely attracted large crowds in Football League division three, south. But the police needed to be on hand to ensure the conditions were met, given the immense enthusiasm for the fixture.

Just one issue overshadowed football as it made a tentative return. Members of the armed forces were refused a discount at the turnstiles. The only way to avoid paying at the gate was to go out and play. Sproston turned out for the Aldershot and Army team. He probably wished he settled on an afternoon watching from the Aldershot terraces.

He endured a bit of a nightmare. A loose back pass to a dozing goalkeeper nearly led to a goal. Everton's Irish full-back, Billy Cook, saved Sproston from embarrassment. But in the second half, a weak challenge on Barnet's Lester Finch contributed to a winner for the FA team. Finch, an amateur, evaded a tackle and outpaced the England international before scoring. The game ended FA XI 1, Aldershot and Army 0.

Proceeds for the game went to the St John Ambulance Brigade and the British Red Cross, a charity Sproston happily worked with for the rest of the war. The *Aldershot News* celebrated a 'brilliant game' of football. Many clever touches delighted the spectators. John MacAdam of the *Daily Express* sniffily dismissed the game as 'dull'. Fans left the game in their army uniform more in agreement with the local newspaper. It was good to see football back with international star players in action.

The following week an Army FA XI lined up against Chelsea at Aldershot. Bert Sproston and Liverpool's Matt Busby united as team-mates for the first time. They built a friendship to endure for the rest of the war and beyond. The army team, an Aldershot Command Eleven, won 4-3. Unfortunately, Sproston scored an own goal.

Soon the home associations of the FA, the Scottish Football Association (SFA), Irish Football Association (IFA) and the Football Association of Wales (FAW) agreed to play internationals between themselves. They arguably treated home internationals as more important than any others, spending the pre-war years stubbornly out of the World Cup. The FA was even invited to take part despite not being a member of FIFA. It refused.

FA boss Stanley Rous took no responsibility for England's infamous salute in Berlin. It was meant to help to prevent war. Rous found another purpose for football in the midst of war. 'Internationals as part of the endeavour to shrug off the discomforts of war, the bombing, the rationing, the restrictions on everyday life,' Rous remembered in his autobiography. 'Just because our lives were so cramped, and because the threat of sudden death was with civilians, as well as soldiers, there was a heightened enjoyment, an uninhibited relish among players and spectators, which made these matches a special experience.'

No caps were awarded for wartime internationals, not even for the so-called victory internationals staged in the immediate aftermath of war. But dozing at his barracks in Aldershot, Bert Sproston received a welcome knock on the door. A telegram from the FA informed him that his services were required for the England team to play at the Racecourse Ground in Wrexham on 18 November 1939. Proceeds from the game went to the Red Cross. There was no longer a simple invitation from the FA to play for England. He needed permission from the army and permission was granted.

The first of these wartime internationals was staged in Cardiff a week earlier. Wales and England drew 1-1. Bert turned up in Wrexham to be reunited with his Manchester City team-mates Frank Swift and Eric Brook. His old friend Stanley Matthews was also waiting in the England dressing room.

Verdicts varied on the game in front of a crowd of approximately 17,000. 'Classic' appeared a tad over-generous. Puzzlement at just how the game was decided in 12 frantic second-half minutes crossed the mind of England's right-back. The *News Chronicle* described Sproston's performance as sound. Arsenal's 2-1 defeat of his old club Spurs in a north London derby at Highbury attracted as much attention. The *Daily Express* conveyed alarm that even with the limits on spectators at sports events, greyhound racing attracted more support than soccer.

Bert's friend Rolf was one of those anxious to see a north London derby. Given that his team lost, he was better off staying on his farm. As for alternative entertainment? The *Daily Express* intimated that football was going to the dogs. His native country had gone to the Nazi dogs, ravaged by them. Why not a visit to watch the greyhounds? He decided to stick with association football.

Nobody believed that the war against Germany might be over by Christmas. Cruel and miserable lessons had been learned since the tragedy of the Great War. Boasts of war being over by Christmas were ridiculed. The first Christmas since the outbreak of World

War II did bring Bert home. Not only did he leave Aldershot but ended up playing at Crewe Alexandra, just down the road from his family home in Sandbach. He was back with Manchester City. No more games for Aldershot for the time being. The bad news was that his mate Matthews was allowed to turn out for Crewe, despite being a player for nearby Stoke City. The good news for Sproston was that Matthews played on the opposite wing.

Bert would have been forgiven for offering a chuckle as he read about speculation over his mate's whereabouts during the Christmas period. Stoke fans became irritated by his perceived lack of loyalty to his hometown club. On this occasion it was not Matthews's fault.

The Potters wanted him to play away at Lincoln City but permission for him to travel was refused by the RAF. As Matthews was based in the Crewe area, he asked for permission to play for 'the Alex'. Stoke City agreed. Manchester City provided opponents, such as Sproston, with international pedigree. But the *Crewe Chronicle*'s headline of 'magnetic Matthews' aptly summed up the reason for a bumper Christmas crowd at Gresty Road of more than 5,000. Crewe's average attendance was well below that number for home matches, even before the war. Matthews agreed to don its red shirt. His presence guaranteed a bumper crowd.

The old friends gave each other a warm welcome in front of an enthusiastic crowd. Matthews brought along another couple of first division ringers from Stoke City – the Potters' diminutive midfielder, Arthur Tutin, and Clement Smith, who was on the brink of retiring from football. Approaching his 30th birthday, the professional game seemed a bit pointless.

Sproston's Manchester City were more or less at full strength. A tight game ensued. Forget Matthews playing for Crewe

Alexandra. The *Crewe Chronicle* found a more important local angle in assessing Alex's opponents. It took care to inform its readers, 'Of special interest was the appearance of the international right-back Sproston, who is a native of Sandbach, and learned the rudiments of the game with the Ramblers.' It credited him with giving one of the best displays. Manchester City won 2-1.

By spring 1940, the Luftwaffe had yet to pound British cities. The Blitz was some months off, so too the Battle of Britain. Maybe it was a time for large crowds to attend sports events again. Such was the confidence among the British authorities, it allowed the 'Hampden roar' to return. The *Scotsman* newspaper urged caution. It speculated that a wartime international between Scotland and England in spring 1940 might be 'the last big sports fixture' for the duration of the war. It was wrong.

A crowd of around 60,000 turned up for the game in Glasgow on 11 May 1940. More than 75,000 tickets had been sold. Proceeds went to the Red Cross. Lord Haw-Haw, William Joyce, was held responsible for the thousands of Scottish supporters failing to turn up for the game. He claimed during one of his infamous propaganda broadcasts from Germany that the game would never go beyond half-time. It grew into false rumours spread throughout the city that the game had been called off altogether. Joyce was hanged after the war for high treason.

Bert Sproston lined up for the final time in an England shirt, albeit one shorn of the three lions. No cap was awarded. Sproston enjoyed a good game despite almost scoring an own goal. It was disallowed by the Scottish referee, William Webb. He also cleared a ball off the line with his chest. The game, a tame affair for the traditional auld enemies, ended up in a 1-1 draw.

International games were played on a haphazard basis for understandable reasons. They were confined to the home nations, founders of the International Football Association Board (IFAB) back in the 19th century. The IFAB still controlled the laws of association football, and still does so in the modern era of billionaire players. Nobody controlled the international game in time of war. British football was never keen on the involvement of the world governing body, FIFA, in peacetime. International co-operation, even during a world war, was at odds with its values. The home nations were content to compete among themselves.

Lovers of the beautiful game came up with another ruse to boost morale, satisfy a hungry public starved of football. The War Ministry decided to sanction a touring Army Football Association team. Its first tour was of Northern Ireland in September 1941.

Bert travelled along with his Manchester City mate Frank Swift. While on tour, Bert quite happily teased his friend, Swifty, over his career choices. Manchester City tore up players' contracts at the outbreak of war. What to do at the end of hostilities? Their professional football careers might be over. Before signing professional forms at Manchester City, the England goalkeeper joined the police as a special constable. He quickly learned that the job was not for him. Manchester, at the time, hardly suffered from traffic congestion. But motorists were not grateful for guidance from PC Swift. He explained, 'On my very first day of traffic point duty, I got everything so muddled that, on the advice of a colleague, I walked away, leaving the traffic to sort itself out! I felt at that moment how many full-backs must have felt when playing against Stanley Matthews.'

Swift played in goal for the army team against Ireland at Windsor Park. Sproston missed out. Frank Considine of Third

Lanark and the Royal Signals took his place. But as planned, he did play in victories against an Irish League team, and an army 'XI' of troops based in Northern Ireland. They were all easy matches.

The oddest was a game of cricket against a District Signals army team at Cliftonville. Bert, a regular with his brothers for Sandbach Cricket Club, took a wicket for his team, who won. No surprise given that his captain was England test cricketer, Denis Compton. The Arsenal footballer and international cricketer helped himself to 66 not out. It was a nice holiday for the men of the APTC. They even casually took a road trip along the north Antrim coast to visit the the Giant's Causeway. Why not? It is a must for all tourists, even in times of conflict.

Major Sloan, the honourable secretary of the British Army Football Association, wrote to the Belfast newspapers thanking Irish fans for their hospitality. 'It is impossible for me, on behalf of my men, to adequately express what we feel in regard to the reception we have received from the public and the troops in the old country,' he commented. 'The lavish hospitality and extreme kindness shown to us all by everybody made this tour the pleasantest we have ever experienced.'

Sproston's form for the higher-profile wartime matches remained strong. He was singled out for praise in a game for the army against an FA XI at Bradford Park Avenue on 9 December 1944. More attention, though, fell on Sproston's friend Matt Busby, the army captain. Once again, British newspapers in their scant sports reports looked forward to England playing Scotland as war came to a close. The game was not due until April 1945.

Albert Booth of the *Daily Herald* was unable to hide his anticipation. He moaned of other matches, 'Repetition of wartime representative football, as opposed to national events, has bred a state of staleness among players and spectators.' England versus Scotland mattered, not games between branches of His Majesty's armed forces and the FA. Busby was certain to play at Hampden. Sproston missed out on an England recall despite being described as of 'exceptionally high standard'.

Once victory in war appeared close to being secured, would crowds still flock to watch something as trivial as a football match? Naysayers questioning the sport's popularity were wrong. It served a valuable purpose. Notwithstanding restrictions, tens of thousands of fans stood on the terraces of Wembley and Hampden Park for wartime matches. As German forces retreated in Europe, victory seemingly assured, eager fans returned to league football grounds in their thousands.

More than 51,000 packed into St James' Park, Newcastle on 10 March 1945 for a game between the Army and the RAF. It was billed as a trial match for the forthcoming match between England and Scotland. But the vast crowd filed out of the ground feeling disappointed after a goalless draw.

North East regional newspaper the *Sunday Sun* declared that many reputations were marred. Despite helping his goalkeeper Frank Swift to keep a clean sheet, Bert hoped, a little forlornly, for a recall to the England team. It was not forthcoming. What became of a promising international career? First it was bedevilled by the routine footballer's curse of injury. Then more fundamentally it ended in war. There were to be no more England call-ups. Just the odd foray with glorified Great Britain teams.

His final experience of international football came in service with the army of the Rhine in Belgium. It almost cost him his life, despite never coming under enemy fire while on tour with the FA and the army football team. An FA XI, captained by Scotland's

Busby, played against the Belgian national team in Brussels. It was in effect Belgium versus Great Britain. Busby was the only Scot. Busby and Sproston's friendship grew as the irascible Scot led the British Army Football Association team. He served as its captain, then the player-manager. It was Busby's first foray into the role of management before taking over as boss at Manchester United after the war.

Football fever gripped the reconquered Belgian capital. Sport served as a welcome relief, especially football. The ground held 30,000 spectators but memories returned of the famous 1923 'White Horse FA Cup Final' as more than 45,000 fans poured into the stadium. Gates were broken down. Hundreds of Allied soldiers as well as civilians encroached on to the pitch. Players had to wade through fans to be able to take throw-ins, goal kicks and corners. The FA XI, effectively a Great Britain team, beat Belgium 3-2 at Stade du Daring Club on 25 March 1945. Tommy Lawton scored a hat-trick.

A fortnight later, the FA sent another representative team to Belgium, this time giving its players an unwelcome reminder of the fragility of 1940s aviation technology. Even without the menace of the Luftwaffe, air flight was still perilous. For professional footballers seconded to military teams, air flight suddenly became the norm. Working-class lads enjoyed the perks of the monied classes of the pre-war years, however perilous by modern standards. Air flights to foreign shores? Yes. As Bert would have seen, not quite the perks. No champagne reception to calm any nerves. 'Strap yourselves in lads,' instead.

Players usually travelled to matches aboard RAF Dakota military transport aircraft. Most had been commandeered for a paratroop airdrop over the Rhine. The FA's touring party of footballers was split up to fly to Liege aboard smaller Anson aircraft. Disaster nearly struck when Bert was on board an Anson flight along with George Hardwick of Middlesbrough and Villa's Les Smith.

As their plane came in to land, the pilot noticed a US Air Force Liberator bomber broken down on the runway. Bert and company sat startled in the body of their plane as it suddenly banked steeply back into the heavens. The pilot had aborted the landing. He flew over and around the control tower before landing safely once the runway was clear. The exhibition games were less eventful, ending 0-0 and 1-1.

The days of exhibition matches were over. Bert and his mates could be forgiven for thinking so, but no. Army bosses were anxious to quench the thirst for football and boost morale. A marathon itinerary for a United Kingdom army touring team visiting the home of the reigning world champions seemed irresistible. The series of battles to defeat fascism in Italy are sometimes derided in history as the 'forgotten campaign'. Both the FA and Army FA wanted to ensure that troops stationed there were not forgotten.

Bert wearily picked up his military orders. A bit different from the FA's invites to represent England in the late 1930s for all their stuffiness. Those also amounted to tickets to a glorified 'holiday'. Instructions for a tour of Italy in May 1945 told the players to gather at the Great Western Railway Hotel in Paddington. They would then be taken to an airfield for the flight to Italy.

The lucky players, including Bert, were informed, 'Uniform will be worn by all ranks and AB 64 [a British soldiers' payment book and identity document] will be carried. If necessary, arrangements will be made for temporary issue in Italy of khaki drill. Baggage is limited to 55lb per man and provision should be made for an adequate supply of towels, soap, razor blades, toothpaste etc. Players will also supply their own football boots. The tour will begin on 6 May and will end on 2 June with the proviso that any players selected to play for England on 26 May will be flown back on 23 or 24 May in time to take part in this match.'

The statement blithely annoyed Scottish players in the army team, most notably the captain Matt Busby. On the day before the touring party was due to convene at a west London hotel, Busby played for a Scottish services team in a 2-2 draw with Hibernian at Easter Road. Along with Andy Black, he headed for London soon after the final whistle. The press was briefed, 'Matt Busby travels principally as team manager and not in his usual role of international half-back.' As Bert Sproston and his team-mates waited in the Paddington hotel, they would be more than justified in thinking they might just be about to greet a future managerial legend. All knew him well.

It was Busby's first foray into the role of management before taking over as boss at Manchester United after the war. The Manchester United role from the club's chief scout, Louis Rocca, came while he was still serving in the army. Rocca wrote to Busby in December 1944 informing him that he had 'a great job offer' in mind for him once the war was over. The devout Italian Catholic told Busby that he was offering him his prayers. He then wished his future recruit 'a lucky New Year'.

Busby described the army role in his autobiography *Soccer at the Top, My Life in Football* as 'I/C, The Army Football Team'. He noted, 'All the players in the team were in the top class of the game. And I quickly realised the importance of delegation.' Cliff Britton was put in charge of transport after Frank Swift and

Tommy Lawton 'borrowed' an army truck to go on a sightseeing tour of Pompeii. Swift and Lawton were assigned the roles of baggage carriers.

Busby stated that Joe Mercer became 'I/C' rations on the basis that his wife's family were in the grocery business. But he had been posted to the Middle East, his army bosses refusing to release him for football games in Italy. By the time a *Daily Mirror* correspondent visited the British army football team in Rome, just after the end of war in Europe, Bert Sproston found himself attending to the rations. Busby proudly declared, 'We ate well.'

Driving around in an army truck on bumpy conditions in the heat of a late Italian spring offered something of a challenge. The games failed to do so. They thrashed their opponents in every game apart from a 2-0 victory over the Naples Area team in Rimini.

Just to bolster their opponents for the final game against an American Fifth Army XI in Florence, the FA recruited several Brazilians serving with their country's armed forces in Italy. Brazil had entered the war on the side of the Allies against the Axis fascist powers in August 1942. It followed a series of attacks on Brazilian merchant shipping by German U-boats throughout summer 1942. More than 25,000 Brazilian troops were deployed to the Italian front. As the war drew to a close, the US 5th Army needed a few 'ringers' from Brazil to join its football team for the game against the British in Florence. It made no difference. The game on 20 May 1945 was won by the British 10-0.

The *Civil and Military Gazette* commented, 'Up to the 32nd minute, when the first goal was scored, there was fast, closely contested, thrill-packed play, but thereafter the superiority of the tourists became increasingly evident and goals came rapidly.'

As Bert packed his boots into his army kit bag in autumn 1939, he would have noted the few naysayers questioning the future of his sport. There were far more important matters as the world went to war than the future of professional football. Yet some critics cried, 'Let football go to the dogs.' Greyhound racing was growing as a spectator sport. Speedway remained popular. There was nothing more quintessentially English than a game of cricket during the summer months. But a war-weary public craved all spectator sport as the war ended, not least Britain's national winter game. Few dared question the future of football and its popularity was assured. Football fans, along with the people of an entire continent, looked forward to a return to normality.

Unfortunately, Bert Sproston, along with many others, lost the best years of his professional career. It was a price he was more than happy to pay. He knew all too well what was at stake, the sacrifices made. Given the global carnage, Bert never considered the suspension of his football dreams to be too much of a problem. Nor did his fellow professionals. The Second World War broke out when he was aged 24 and finally ended in August 1945 when he was 30. For professional footballers of the era, those missing years would have been his most fruitful.

Brian James, a leading football correspondent of the day, wrote in his history of Anglo-Scottish football, *England v Scotland*, 'Those years took great bites out of the career span of some of the greatest players these islands ever produced. The mere fact of the concurrent world conflict should not deprive them of their credit, for it does not disguise the evidence of their talent.' James pointed to England's fine form in wartime internationals with two or three dozen different players as evidence of the world class talent on offer. The embarrassing performance of England at the 1950 World Cup and their humiliating 6-3 defeat to Hungary in 1953 put paid to any of those premature notions of world supremacy.

Once victory was declared in Europe, Bert Sproston rested in his barracks on the outskirts of Rome to reflect on what remained of his football career. Stanley Matthews was a freak. Not too many players went much beyond the age of 30 playing domestic, let alone international football. During the course of his international career, he unwittingly became a young boy's saviour from the Nazis. He also served as a soldier and part-time footballer. Little did Bert realise but the military career of the German refugee he saved in Berlin also brought him to Belgium in a British military uniform.

It was not as easy for the German refugee to sign up for the British army as the England football international. Britain offered the Jewish refugee sanctuary. Joining His Majesty's armed forces? To be blunt, he was German. Put simply, he was not trusted.

ROLF/RALPH'S WAR

HOW MIGHT Rolf confront the Nazis in war? How might he 'do his bit' for his adopted country – one at war with the land of his birth? 'I will join the British army,' thought Rolf on the declaration of war. He needed to think again as it was not so simple. Britain was desperate for military manpower, fresh recruits. Professional footballers, such as Bert Sproston, were fine. But not everyone suited the demands of the Ministry of War.

Ostensibly, Rolf's credentials were impeccable. As a German Jew, he had first-hand experience of the consequences of the Nazis' evil doctrine. For any covert military roles, he spoke the German language fluently. Listed by the British authorities as stateless, he was still German. He was no Nazi but suspicions lingered. Anti-Semitism existed in England. Not everybody was as tolerant and humane as Bert Sproston. Anti-German hatred, barely abated in the aftermath of World War One, returned vigorously. The British hated anyone they considered to be a 'hun'.

An opportunity arose. A British army regiment took in German and Austrian young men, who had fled the Nazis. More specifically, it recruited Jewish refugees. As a general rule, the armed forces still distrusted anti-Nazi refugees from the European mainland to the extent of discouraging recruitment into any frontline combat rules. No chance of Rolf following his friend Bert into the tank corps.

The British Army's Pioneer Corps designated its troops as non-combatants although still vital. The bravery of its men was rarely in question. Their role was to supply armaments and food to frontline troops, carry out engineering works and help to co-ordinate logistics. They were affectionately known as 'The King's most loyal enemy aliens'.

The historian, Helen Fry, estimates that Rolf was among 10,000 Germans and Austrians signing up to fight for Britain. That amounted to almost one in seven of the 75,000 refugees, who sought sanctuary from Nazi oppression in the United Kingdom up until the outbreak of war. Some of them even fought for Germany against Britain in the First World War.

Rolf spotted the opening. He considered serving with the Pioneer Corps as ideal albeit perilous work. Most of his young life was spent living in peril. Just after the declaration of war, labour companies of reservists amalgamated to form the Auxiliary Military Pioneer Corps (AMPC). Rolf signed up but as a reservist, he was yet to go to war.

Just one important problem needed to be overcome. He always feared a knock on the door from uniformed men in Berlin. Unfortunately for a Jewish kid living in Berlin it became the norm. But a knock on the door from officials in England or Scotland? It seemed irrational. 'This is ridiculous,' Rolf mused to himself. 'So much for the Nazis rounding up Jews, so much for their special branch interrogating Jews. The British are doing the same! An enemy alien? I wanted to escape the Nazi enemy.'

Not once but twice he was called before a detention board. Paranoia descended on a troubled nation. The British right-wing press singled out German Jews for suspicion. No matter that they were being persecuted under Hitler's totalitarian rule. Worse still, murdered.

Thousands of German refugees were interned by the British authorities as 'enemy aliens'. They included Rolf's dad. He was interned on the Isle of Man. After spending his formative years avoiding Nazi detention, Rolf suddenly ended up before a British panel considering whether to lock him up. Good references were needed to avoid detention. He had one of the best in the guise of references from an England international footballer. How much the name Bert Sproston impressed his special branch interrogators is open to question. It was certainly unusual.

Rolf first faced his interrogators as he worked as a trainee at Torr farm near Rhu in Dumbartonshire. The best policy was just simply to co-operate. Answer questions openly and honestly. The Scottish police may be football fans so perhaps it was best not to mention his friend, the England defender Bert Sproston.

Then again, give it a go. Why not? The panel ruled on 23 November 1939 that he would be exempt from registration for internment while serving in the AMPC. Relief for Ralph. He was bluntly described on the panel's notes as 'a stateless refugee from Nazi oppression'.

A move back to southern England brought him once again under suspicion, despite still being a reservist with the AMPC. It was June 1940. Members of the corps had been deployed in the ill-fated Battle of France. Rolf was also on the move, working as a farm trainee at the village of Burpham near Guildford in Surrey. It was there that he was able to see his mother for the first time in more than four years.

Then came the knock on the door from Surrey Police. Interrogators seemed unimpressed by the typewritten description of stateless. Rolf, reasonably, feared that they wanted to intern him. One of them scrawled 'German' in red ink across the card for his interrogation. He even wrote, 'consider alternatives'. Rolf, reasonably, feared that they wanted to intern him. Fortunately, the farmer intervened. Friedland was needed for agricultural work and would not be much use to the war effort sat in a camp for interned detainees.

The panel meeting on 20 June 1940 simply recorded him as a Jewish refugee, one considered satisfactory. Unlike their colleagues in Scotland, there was no specific nod to him fleeing the Nazi peril. Maybe they did take notice of his references. Maybe one of them just happened to be a Manchester City fan, an admirer of their expensive signing, Bert Sproston. Doubtful that he was a Spurs fan.

Unlike his dad, Rolf escaped detention by the British and overcame any subliminal hostility towards him. Indeed, the UK authorities released most German refugees detained in British camps by the autumn of 1940. Only those suspected of links to the Nazis remained under lock and key.

Only one enemy remained in the mind of Rolf Friedland. It was not the British. His boss reflected the ordinary British mindset, rather than the officious Surrey cops. His experience at their hands was just a little chastening. He went to the recruitment office in Guildford and asked to go full-time. The recruiting officer happily granted the request, sending him to a month of basic training with the pioneers at Ilfracombe in north Devon. He set his sights on the German enemy.

To do so, he needed just a simple change of a noticeably German-Jewish name to just plain English. He opted for Ralph

Freeman. He had met men with one or other of the names. It seemed a decent English and Christian approximation to his German identity. There were a couple of reasons to adopt the moniker. Firstly, the distinctly middle-class name might help to better integrate into British society. Secondly, in case of capture by the Nazis. For the moment he remained simply as Rolf, the boy implausibly pleading for freedom to an English footballer outside Berlin's Olympic stadium.

His first posting was with the Pioneer Corps' 248 Company at Catterick camp in Yorkshire. From there he joined number 88 Company at the Sennybridge camp in the Brecon Beacons. A welcome period of leave spent near to the Mumbles in south Wales left a profound impression on him. One of its tourist spots, Langland Bay, is dangerously attractive, especially to surfers. As someone only used to messing about with boats on a river in landlocked Berlin, Rolf worked out that the sea can be your enemy, not your friend.

Much about the war he was unable to relate to his family. Events in Langland Bay remained etched in his memory. 'Surely no one can be in peril in such a beautiful peaceful sport,' he mused as the waves crashed into the shore. A cry came from near to distant rocks. His fellow beach-goers pointed out to sea, yelling in despair. Someone, anyone, needed to save a boy in distress. Rolf told his family in later years that he intuitively assessed the situation and dived in.

A thought flashed through his mind, reminders of his lonely perilous days in Berlin. An athlete saved his life. His pace quickened as he ran through the breeze and stepped into the rollers hitting the sandy beach. 'I know that fear, that helplessness. But what can I do? What if I fail?' As soon as he began churning through the waters, just like the boy swimming and boating in Berlin, those doubts vanished.

Cross the white line in football, there is simply a game to be played. Nerves mostly disappear. Just wait for the referee's whistle. Cross the reclining tideline in search of a drowning boy, no room for nerves, no room for doubts. A saviour delivered him from his enemy and now it was his turn to be a saviour. Someone, not anyone, took a chance on him – he needed to do the same.

Rolf grabbed the sobbing boy. He struggled against the powerful current in Langland Bay and pulled the frightened young lad to shore. They crawled out of the sea and on to the sand. Screaming onlookers ran towards them, one yelling loudly for a medic. Both Rolf and the boy seemed fine despite their ordeal.

As they caught their breath on the beach, one member of the gathering crowd gave them a blanket. She told Rolf that he was a hero. Shaking his head he told her, 'No. I'm not a hero. I just did what I had to do.' His own hero was a footballer, who did what he had to do. A footballer by the name of Bert Sproston, who was by then deployed abroad in war.

For all Rolf's modesty, his act of heroism brought him royal recognition. His commanding officer stood before him holding a scroll. The citation was from the king's brother, Prince Henry, Duke of Gloucester, president of the Royal Humane Society. It read, 'For your brave and selfless act of saving a life, you are hereby awarded a special citation, signed by His Royal Highness, the Duke of Gloucester.'

Rolf's son Alan told me, 'This moment is symbolic for him – it marks a turning point where he begins to see himself as part of British society. The name change to Ralph Freeman represents his decision to fully embrace his new identity and leave behind the fear and trauma of his past.'

Like any German refugee he fell under suspicion. MI5 tracked his movements even as a member of His Majesty's Armed Forces. The file on Rolf Friedland/Ralph Freeman's application for British citizenship held at the UK National Archives was closed until 2048. It was opened after a Freedom of Information request revealing the following from MI5, 'Our records show that in December 1942 the applicant was a member of the committee of the Catterick Cultural Centre, an organisation known to be largely controlled by communists. We have, however, no evidence of any political or undesirable activity, and apart from the foregoing, we have nothing recorded against him.'

Never mind that at that stage of the war Britain was an ally of the totalitarian communist state of the Soviet Union. Hitler's catastrophic miscalculation by tearing up his pre-war deal with Stalin and ordering an invasion brought the British and Russians together. Communist dogma no longer mattered but suspicions lingered. Mistrust of communists, especially those with Soviet links, would return in the post-war era. No matter, the British spooks had nothing recorded against Rolf Friedland/Ralph Freeman other than his trips to a northern English working men's club.

His military record shows that the frightened teenage German refugee served impeccably in His Majesty's Armed Forces during the war. Ralph's commanding officer supported his application for British citizenship. It noted that he had been awarded a 'testimonial by the Royal Humane Society for assisting to save a schoolboy from the sea at Langland Bay, Swansea'. His son Alan said, 'My father certainly had no communist sympathies whatsoever. He did have a strong social conscience but that's it really. I suspect that the appeal of that group was probably because they were strongly anti-Nazi.'

Ralph Freeman just happened to be one of hundreds of thousands in the Allied armed forces waiting for the signal to invade. It depended on the weather readings, crucially one from an Irish lighthouse. Nowhere in Britain or France is battered by the Atlantic weather more than County Mayo in neutral Ireland. As a lone soul in Berlin, he would have felt some sympathy and empathy for the loneliness of lighthouse keepers off the Irish Atlantic coast. It was bleak, the risk of being marooned and abandoned. But there was always the chance of rescue. He would certainly appreciate their dedication, fortitude and stoicism.

In early June 1944, the barometer readings fell. The change in air pressure helped to relax the blood pressure of Group Captain James Stagg, the Royal Air Force's weather forecaster. He advised a delay in the Normandy invasion, slated for 5 June 1944, partly on the basis of weather readings being sent from Ireland. Given more readings from Blacksod in Ireland, he advised that conditions might be favourable for 6 June 1944.

Ralph's chance had come. He was about to confront the enemy. He was German, a refugee fighting alongside the British. The ranks of Wehrmacht, SS storm troopers and Panzer divisions were an alien enemy to many of those barracked in military Nissen huts along England's Channel coast. To him, the evil of the Nazis, its goose-stepping fanatics, was all too familiar. Toiling on the land, helping to bring food to a British populace living on meagre rationed supplies felt good. He wanted to do more; confront the very people he escaped from just a few years earlier.

The Normandy landings on 6 June 1944 were a success. Ralph was made to wait. Tactically, the Germans were caught unaware, believing that Allied forces would land further north on the French coast. They still put up fierce resistance. The Royal Pioneer Corps boasts today, 'The true glory of the war against Fascism belonged to the ordinary soldier; to the Infantryman, the mechanised Trooper, the Sapper, the Driver, the Pioneer.'

In all, 13 companies of Pioneers landed on the beaches in the first wave of attacks, with a further ten in the next wave of attacks on D-Day – some 19,000 men. The first of them are believed to have landed on the beaches around 20 minutes after the start of Operation Overlord. They faced varying levels of resistance, mines taking out landing craft. Snipers made work on the beaches near impossible. As the day progressed, they began clearing the beaches of casualties, before lying lateral track, constructing wheeled and track exits for the heavy equipment about to be landed.

As the Allied invasion forces on D-Day consolidated their positions, Pioneers began building the temporary Mulberry docks. In common with his comrades, it was some weeks before Ralph crossed the Channel. It was not just German resistance to blame – the weather once again intervened. Normandy's coast was battered by gale force winds. More than 800 naval vessels were lost, including landing craft.

In July 1944, he finally landed on the beaches of Arromanches in Normandy with the 137th Armoured Division. The Mulberry dock nearing completion on Arromanches somehow held despite the fierce storm, a credit to the skills of his Pioneer comrades. Just one oddity, as the fighting raged, Ralph momentarily suffered flashbacks to the day he escaped Berlin – images of the streets, the German officers, above all his feelings of desperation flickered through his mind. 'I wasn't supposed to survive in Nazi Berlin,' Ralph told his family. 'But there I was on the Normandy beaches.'

Bert Sproston begins his final season for Leeds United versus Charlton Athletic, 28 August 1937

Ralph Freeman enlisted for the British Army, Ilfracombe, Devon, 1941 (Credit: Freeman family)

England's football team (white shirts) make the Nazi salute alongside the Germany team, Berlin, 14 May 1938

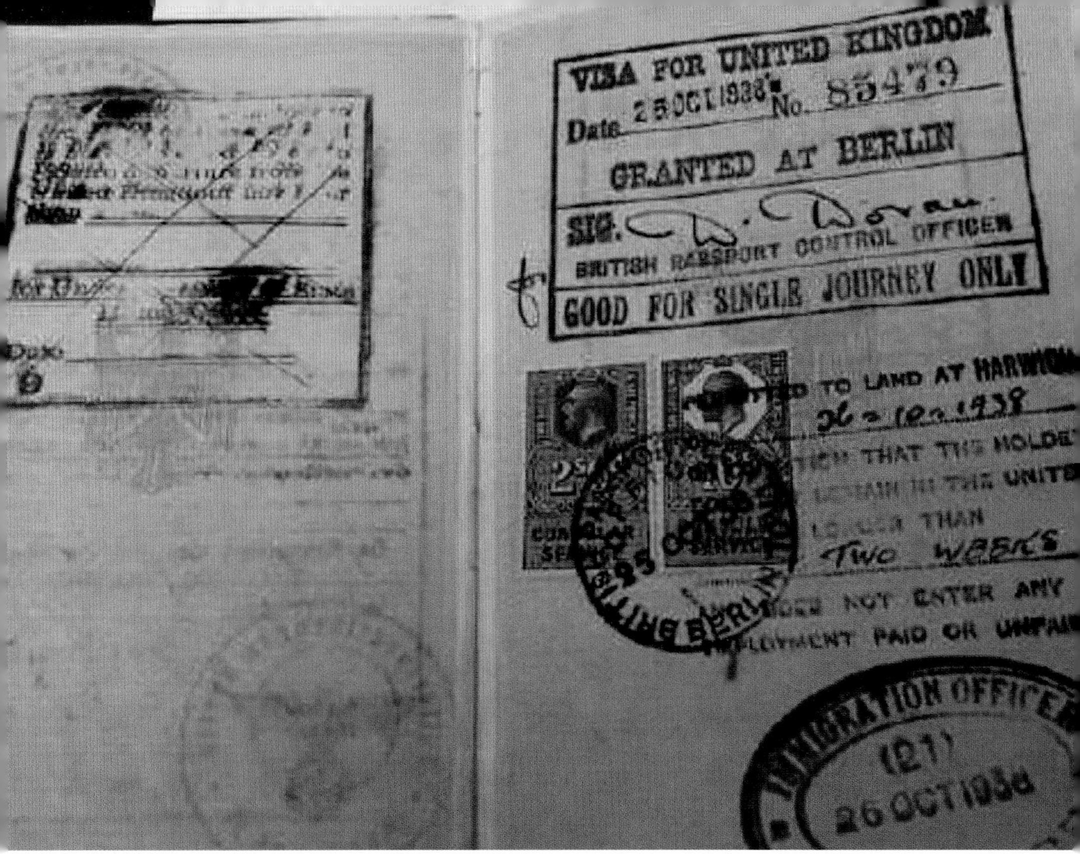

Visa issued to Rolf Friedland at the British Embassy in Berlin for travel to Harwich, England on 26 October 1938 (Courtesy, Alan Freeman)

An undated photograph of Rolf Friedland, later Ralph Freeman (top row, third from left), with his football team in Berlin. (Courtesy Alan Freeman)

England players, including Bert Sproston with Stanley Matthews behind him, walk out for a game against France in Paris, 26 May 1938

Sproston's final international game abroad for England. France 2 England 4, 26 May 1938, Stade de Colombes, Paris

Bert Sproston making his Spurs debut in a 'friendly' match against Arsenal challenges Welsh international Bryn Jones, 21 August 1938

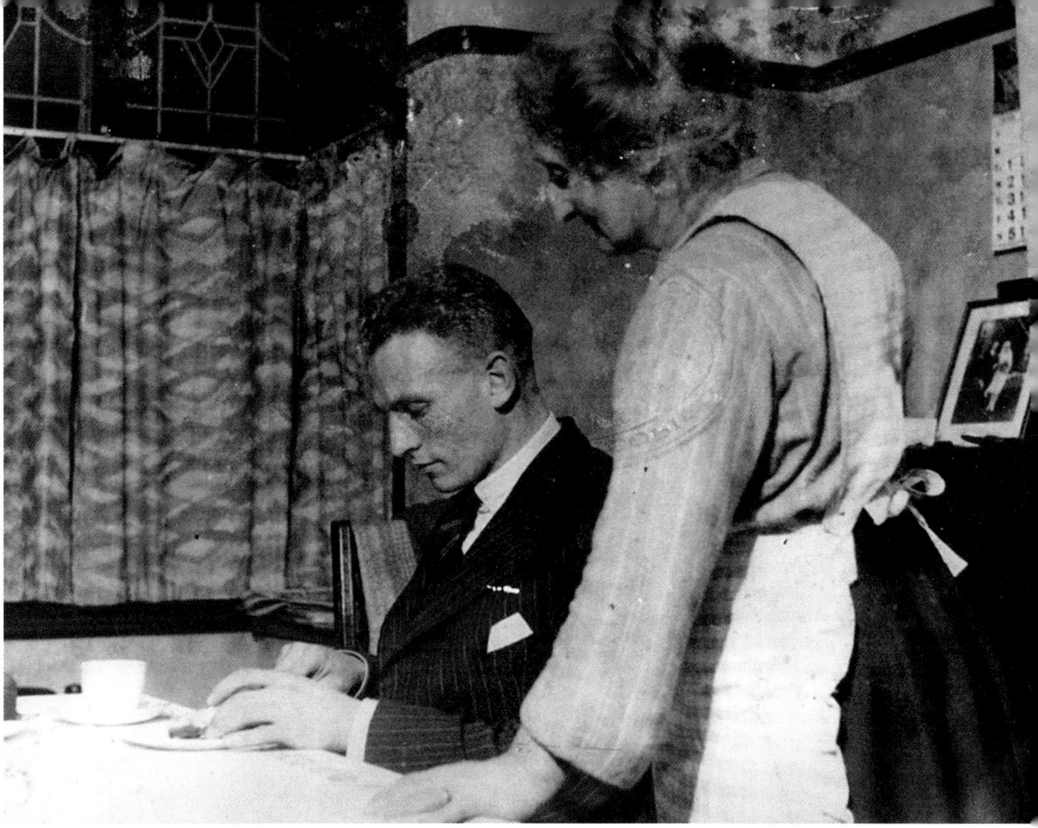

Alice Sproston oversees her son Bert signing for Manchester City (Courtesy: Sproston family)

The British Army football squad goes on tour for the first time. It is a tour of Northern Ireland, 1941. Bert Sproston is second from the right in the back row (Picture: British Army Football Association)

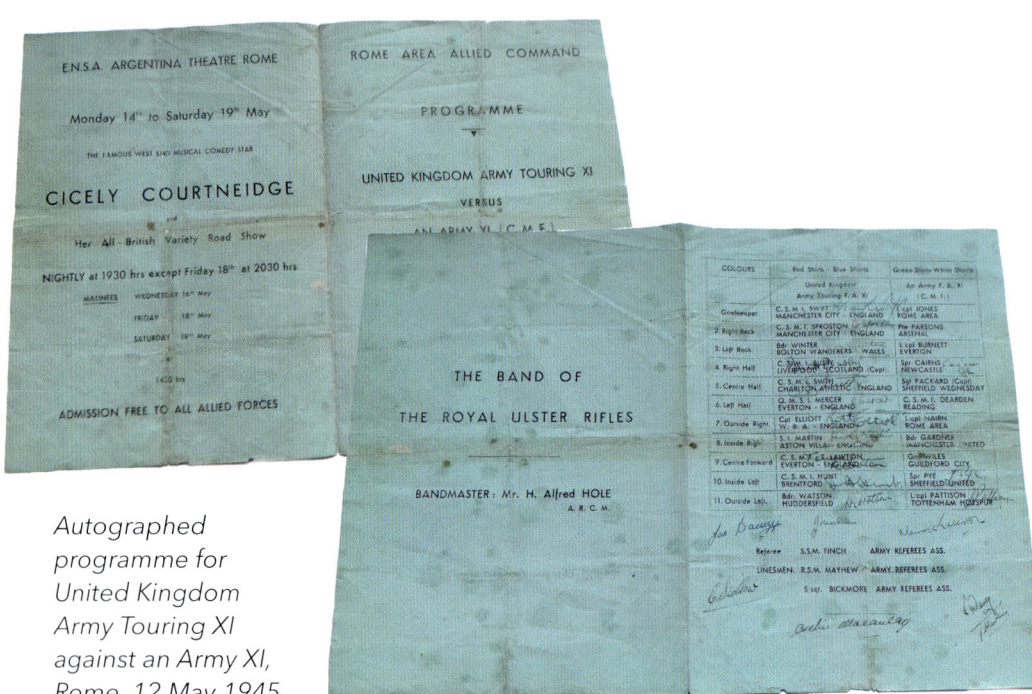

Autographed
programme for
United Kingdom
Army Touring XI
against an Army XI,
Rome, 12 May 1945.
Sproston plays for the
UK Army Touring XI (Picture: British Army Football
Association)

Manchester City captain
Bert Sproston (left)
shakes hands with
Manchester United's
Johnny Carey at Maine
Road. Mr C Fletcher
of Northwich refereed
the Manchester derby
wearing a jacket and
shorts, a high neck,
unbuttoned shirt with
arms folded back
and a pocket hankie.
It ended 0-0. Maine
Road, Manchester, 20
September 1947

Bert Sproston checks the Bolton Wanderers kit before the 1958 FA Cup Final

In the dugout for Bolton Wanderers FC, Bert Sproston during his first season as the club's trainer. In the background is John Higgins, a member of the 1958 FA Cup winning team (Picture: Bolton Wanderers FC)

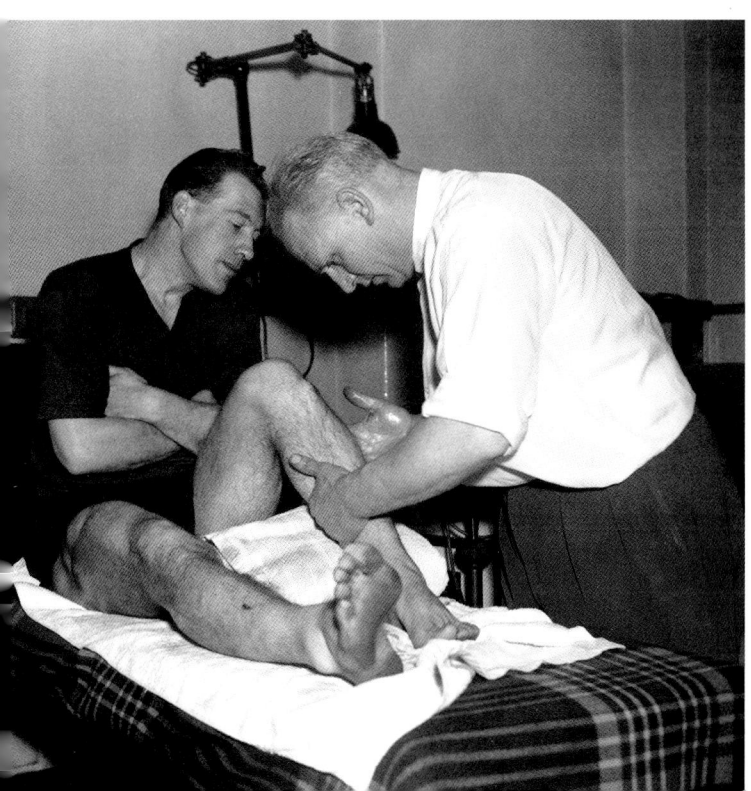

Bolton Wanderers trainer Bert Sproston works on the injured leg of the team's skipper, Nat Lofthouse, at Burnden Park on 22 February 1959

Bolton Wanderers proudly displaying the FA Cup and the FA Charity Shield. (Back rowk l-r) Roy Hartle, John Higgins, Bryan Edwards, Eddie Hopkinson, Derek Hennin, Tommy Banks and Bert Sproston (trainer). (Front row l-r) Brian Birch, Dennis Stevens, Nat Lofthouse, Bill Ridding (manager), Raymond Parry, Douglas Holden and Ralph Gubbins

Bert Sproston (Courtesy the Sproston Family/ Manchester City FC)

The Royal Pioneers' Corps Association records, 'A Pioneer Group and four companies were regularly employed on unloading ships from Mulberry – the prefabricated port – and three companies were operating Dukes. Other companies were erecting tentage for Casualty Clearing Stations and General Hospitals or setting up Bailey bridging; some were used in REME workshops repairing landing craft and tanks, and on the responsible task of signposting and traffic control. The men bivouacked in fields, in unusually harsh weather, working extremely long hours with little rest.'

Rolf's 137th Division of Pioneers set about finishing off the Mulberry dock before repairing roads and communication networks around the besieged city of Caen. British forces failed to dislodge German forces, despite unleashing a fierce bombardment. It took weeks for the historic city to fall as Allied forces broke out of Normandy. Even then Rolf's war almost came to a premature end at Normandy's Falaise Gap. Soldiers deemed it the 'pocket of death'.

German troops regrouped at Falaise. Halting the Allied invaders there would seriously hamper attempts to recapture the rest of France. The Germans failed but not before a sniper spotted young Ralph. He shot him. Ralph spent the next few weeks in a field hospital with his wounded left arm strapped in bandages – another lucky escape.

The doctor told him, 'Could've been a lot worse. The bullet missed the bone.' Ralph replied, 'Doesn't feel like it missed by much.' As the doctor moved away, Ralph leant back on his pillow, pausing as he stared across the makeshift ward. According to his family he reflected, 'Another close call. I've had too many of those. First Berlin, now this. Lucky to be alive. How much longer can I keep dodging bullets?'

Just as well that one of the tasks for his Pioneers was building field hospitals. Not only building them, but ensuring supplies of medicines, food and fresh supplies of running water.

It was by no means the end of Ralph's war. Canadian forces led the Allies in the Battle of Scheldt, named after a river flowing between Antwerp and the North Sea. Polish units and the British Army's Pioneer Corps supported them but their battle in October 1944 was made more difficult by the failure of Operation Market Garden, the ill-fated Allied military adventure going down as a 'Bridge Too Far' at Arnhem.

Once again, Ralph enjoyed a lucky escape, his third. The first in Berlin after rescue thanks to Bert Sproston, the next at the battle for Falaise in Normandy, and the final one even after the capture of Antwerp. It was time for a rest. His friend Laufer, another Jewish refugee from Berlin, who was recruited into the British Army, wanted to go to the cinema. They were childhood friends. Ralph told him to go. He decided to stay in barracks, not much bothered with cinema as the Nazis had barred Jews from going to Berlin's picture houses. Given that the movies on offer were riddled with political propaganda it hardly served as punishment. Jewish self-help groups did organise movie showings but Rolf stuck to sport.

Antwerp had been secured by November 1944 but it was certainly not safe. The people of London felt briefly lulled into a false sense of security as the Luftwaffe finally abandoned its Blitz of the British capital. Then came the V1 or 'doodle bugs', then the V2 rockets.

On 16 December 1944, a V2 was fired from Hellendoorn in the Netherlands. Its launch coincided with the beginning of the Ardennes offensive – the so-called 'Battle of the Bulge', Hitler's last desperate throw of the dice. He ordered a counter-attack on the Franco-German border. V2 attacks on British forces in the port of Antwerp, aimed at cutting off supplies and reinforcements, served as more than a distraction.

Rolf's friend Laufer went off to the Rex cinema to watch *The Plainsman*, a Cecil B. DeMille western movie starring Gary Cooper. It was set in the aftermath of the US Civil War. Belgium was in the middle of war. The V2 rocket from the Netherlands struck Antwerp's Rex cinema at De Keyserlei 15 in Antwerp. The cinema was packed with approximately 1,100 customers. It killed 567 people, including 267 members of the Allied armed forces. Laufer was one of them, hundreds of others were injured.

Ralph lost relatives in the Nazi death camps as he discovered after the war – suspected during the war. The possibility of losing a friend to a Nazi missile while watching a Gary Cooper western never crossed his mind. Time for revenge? Not for a disciplined member of His Majesty's Armed Forces. It was not possible anyhow.

Confronting the enemy face-to-face, eye-to-eye, turned out to be a different matter. Once Allied victory was secured, thousands of Germans needed interrogating, not just the surviving members of the Nazi leadership. Trusted German interpreters were needed. Ralph was posted to the 21st Army interpreters' pool. It also meant an attachment to field security in the Royal Welsh Fusiliers. Finally, he met his Nazi tormentors but not as a cowering, fearful Jewish teenager. Now on a human level, he was in charge of them.

Interrogations did not always go well. SS boss Heinrich Himmler infamously managed to swallow a poison pill as he awaited interrogation, escaping justice. Familiar figures in Nazi German sport also faced interrogation. These included a man familiar to Bert Sproston, Germany's national team manager Sepp Herberger. Just a reminder that as England's footballers made the Nazi salute in Berlin's Olympiastadion, Herberger stood appalled. He hid his disgust from both his Nazi masters and their British establishment guests.

American servicemen interrogated Herberger after the war. They concluded he was no Nazi. They were right. Herberger went on to manage West Germany – winning the 1954 World Cup in Switzerland. It was controversial, given suspicions that his players took a performance-enhancing drug, Pervitin, during half-time of the final against Hungary. The drug, an amphetamine, had been refined by Nazi scientists. It was nicknamed 'panzer chocolate'. Herberger booked his place in history as a World Cup-winning manager, regardless of suspicions emerging years after the final whistle at Bern in Switzerland.

Another senior German sports figure escaped sanction from his interrogators. Unlike Herberger, Guido von Mengden was a guilty man. Maybe if Ralph Freeman acted as interpreter in his interrogation, Von Mengden might have been locked up. He was an enthusiastic press officer with the German Football Association, the DFB, during the Nazi era. There's little doubt of Von Mengden's Nazi sympathies. He was a committed Nazi. But as Uli Hesse points out in *Tor!*, Von Mengden managed to fool Allied military personnel carrying out denazification tests and tribunals after the war.

Quite remarkably, he remained one of the most influential figures in German sport right up until the ill-fated Olympic Games of Munich in 1972. And yet this controversial figure once infamously wrote that National Socialism 'has restored the meaning of sport' and 'footballers are political soldiers of the

Führer'. He was not quite one of the men suitable to help run the 'Friendly Games' of Munich – perhaps one reason why it ended up in tragedy.

Football fan Ralph was just a soldier, not a political soldier. Nor for that matter were, at least willingly, members of the team he watched in Berlin on a hot May Day in 1938. Not least among them Sgt Bert Sproston. Ralph earned promotion to the rank of sergeant as he moved to the intelligence unit to assist with interrogations. Unlike the beginning of war, the British deemed fluency in German and first-hand, terrifying knowledge of the Nazis vital at the end of the war.

His son Alan reflected, 'Dad, now in a position of power, faced a symbolic confrontation with the past he left behind. The scene of him interrogating Nazi prisoners highlighted the irony of dad's journey – from a Jewish teenager fleeing Nazi Germany to an interrogator questioning the very people who oppressed him.' The tables had turned.

His British officers, some of them half-amused by the irony of the situation, more or less gave him free rein. As a general rule, more than one member of Allied forces interrogated Nazi suspects. Both would speak German. There was a need for harshness, just no brutality. A challenging task Ralph embraced. At times he sharply told them he had read the intelligence reports on his suspects. He remembered men like them, used to hide from them. They had the power then. At least they did until he escaped courtesy of an English footballer.

Ralph was not like them. He was no Nazi, no Soviet persecutor either. He was a Jew – a target of their hatred. Ralph just wanted to act as a decent human being. During the war he fought alongside other Jews, Christians, Muslims, Hindus, Sikhs, Buddhists and those of no faith at all. Many nationalities together, ethnicities fighting Nazi inhumanity.

Little did he know until after the war but among those members of the US 3rd Army fighting the Nazis from Normandy to Germany just happened to be his brother, Hans. He changed his name to John. The pair were reunited near Düsseldorf with both on duty for their respective new country's denazification units. There was time for a family photo, one proud German Jew in his British army uniform, the other in American uniform.

A chance for revenge from the Friedland brothers? Ralph would simply later tell his friends, 'I used to be the one who looked over my shoulder, terrified. I was just a kid, running for my life, while they [the Nazis] marched through the streets like kings.' At least he did so until rescued by a humane, determined professional footballer from Sandbach in Cheshire with a penchant for steak and kidney puddings. Sergeant Sproston ended the war looking for promotion – Manchester City were going up.

PROMOTION FOR
SERGEANT SPROSTON

THE WORLD war was almost over. A nation celebrated on 8 May 1945; VE Day, victory in Europe, was declared. Hitler was dead. Many of the Nazi leadership were dead – scores of them faced their interrogators. They faced justice and the hangman awaited.

Ralph Freeman was working for the interrogation teams, no time for VE Day celebrations. Bert Sproston knew all too well that any celebrations of his own needed to be put on hold. The war against Japan was not yet over. After his tour of Italy with the army's FA, he served in the Far East. Manchester City credited him with doing 'valuable' work on troop ships. Once on shore, he worked as a physical training instructor to troops garrisoned in India. VJ Day, victory over Japan, eventually came on 15 August 1945.

Even then it did not come until after the horrors of the atom bombs at Hiroshima and Nagasaki. More than 200,000 Japanese citizens were killed and Japan surrendered to the American-led forces. Fears of atomic or nuclear weapons became ingrained in the public psyche.

The Soviet Union, a wartime ally, was the new enemy. Its communist doctrine fuelled light-hearted fears of 'reds under the bed'. Lifting morale remained a priority and football more than helped.

Bert won accolades and international honours as a footballer, albeit without major domestic honour. Few did. There were just two domestic trophies to be won during Sproston's career, the FA Cup and the Football League championship. The FA Cup was considered by many fans of the era as the more prestigious of the two. There was no European club competition for English clubs. The greatest honour was to play for your country and he cherished his England caps.

As his playing career entered its twilight years, there was some unfinished business for Bert. He had signed for Tottenham Hotspur, then Manchester City, before the war with the aim of helping them regain their top-flight status. Neither had done so. Manchester City fans yearned for a return of the glory years. Bert and his team-mates eventually obliged.

Wartime service, though, put any success on the football field into perspective. One of his proudest accolades came from the people of his own hometown of Sandbach. As he looked forward to being demobbed, they presented him with a certificate honouring his service in the war. The citation read, 'The townspeople of Sandbach present to Bert Sproston this certificate in appreciation and gratitude for the devoted service you have rendered in the course of freedom and justice for the benefit of humanity generally. Your contribution to victory is a source of pride to your fellow townsmen and on their behalf the [Sandbach] Urban District Council tenders to you sincere thanks.' Nobody even knew of his rescue of a German-Jewish refugee long before the first shots were fired in the war.

Just how to return to normality post-war? For all the snobbishness towards football from certain quarters, mostly those establishment figures forcing England's futile Hitler salute before the war, few doubted its value. The British public maintained their love of the sport during the war and yearned for more. Bert needed just one last hurrah before his playing days were over.

Theoretically, a resumption of competitive domestic league football after a seven-year break would cheer up fans, players and club owners alike. In reality, these were anything but normal times for football or wider society, little to cheer – brutally so, for Britain's wartime leader, Winston Churchill. He called a general election, expecting an easy victory. A grateful nation rejected him and his Conservative and Unionist party. Churchill was a great wartime leader. But in peacetime the British people were in the mood for a radical new and progressive society.

Optimism filled hearts and minds. Surely, as the British public looked forward to a bold new future, professional football would play its part. Unfortunately, the sport was run by conservative figures. Not necessarily politically but most certainly socially and economically. A few malevolent figures in the national game of football eyed an opportunity for enrichment. The voracious demand for the game from spectators paying at the gate meant pound note signs lit up in their eyes.

Fans not only stumped up cash at the turnstiles. Their ration books were not safe – clubs put out appeals for extra clothing coupons in order to replace shabby and torn playing kit. Player loyalty was also too often taken for granted, if not disregarded. For all his service to club and country, Bert Sproston ended up grovelling for retirement benefits. More on those travails later but first a tragedy at a club he eventually made his footballing home.

The *Daily Herald*'s Clifford Webb gloomily warned, 'I have heard it said in soccer circles quite recently, "We are in for a boom.

The crowds will turn up whatever football they see." Football has a hold on the public, but it is no unbreakable iron grip. Entertaining play from contented players should be a number one priority.' Unfortunately, fans and players being taken for granted seemed to be the order of the day, especially to a large degree, as today, supporters paying through the turnstiles.

There was no darker example of this disdain for fans, the working-class masses flocking to football grounds, than the Burnden Park disaster on 9 March 1946. In the annals of football history, it seems a long-forgotten tragedy, though not in the minds of Bolton Wanderers and Stoke City supporters. Nor to those such as Bert who eventually dedicated his post-playing life to Bolton Wanderers.

Stanley Matthews lined up in the FA Cup quarter-final for Stoke, dreaming of Wembley. As will be explored later, Bert savoured Wembley glory with Bolton in the aftermath of the Munich air disaster. Not before being a losing part of the 'Matthews final'. But the Burnden Park disaster already had a profound impact on the people of his adopted hometown of Bolton, not least the football club with which he forged a firm bond.

A post-war generation had experienced enough tragedy, witnessed enough horrors, suffered personal loss. Footballers, the majority called up for the services, were no different. It was peacetime, a football match, a day to enjoy, cheer, jeer and above all relax. Naturally, the horrific events of the day would have a profound effect on anyone there, even for those who did not know any of the victims.

Just as at Bradford, and Hillsborough some four decades later, fans going along happily to an English football ground, men, women and children, ought to have returned home safely. The tragic fact they did not, the scandal of the authorities failing to learn lessons, instead continuing to treat the national sport, a working-class sport, with disdain verging on contempt, is a source to all of immense shame.

Unusually, it was the second leg of an FA Cup quarter-final. Bolton won the first leg at the Victoria Ground in Stoke 2-0 a week earlier. There was no competitive league action in that post-war season, just the FA Cup. As a result, and critics claimed for financial greed, the FA decreed that cup matches had to be played over two legs, rather than one as was the normal practice. If the tie had been run on traditional lines, the game would never have taken place, as Stoke would have already been knocked out by Bolton.

Nevertheless, the game did go ahead with tragic consequences. Despite playing poorly at home and losing, Stoke's players felt confident for the return leg. 'After all, we had a good side,' commented the team's young captain Neil Franklin in his recollections of the match. 'We had the one and only Stanley Matthews, so we felt there was still some fight left in us.' Stoke fans agreed with them. They made the short trip north from the Potteries to Bolton in their thousands. Bolton fans, confident of victory, also turned up in their tens of thousands.

On arriving at the ground, the Stoke players noted the thousands cramming the streets and packed into the car park outside the main stand of Burnden Park. It was clear they could not all get in. It did not help that one of the stands was closed, commandeered by the government as a storage dump during the war. It had not yet been handed back for the use of its owners, Bolton Wanderers. Thousands of football fans would miss an eagerly anticipated game. They turned out to be the lucky ones. By the end of the day, 33 fans had been killed, hundreds injured.

Estimates put the crowd that day at more than 85,000. But the ground's official capacity was almost 20,000 less. The average crowd for the 1945/46 season had been 43,000. The police and the ground authorities were simply unable to cope.

Accounts of how fans managed to get into Burnden Park after the gates were closed differ. It is not in dispute that many sneaked in via the railway running past the back of the ground, removing the flimsy fencing as they did so. In an eerie echo of the Hillsborough disaster four decades later, it was also alleged others stormed the gates, yet there is no evidence they did so. Within seconds of the referee George Dutton blowing the whistle for the kick-off, two barriers gave way with deathly consequences. The players and officials eventually trooped off the field.

For 20 minutes the players sat in their respective dressing rooms waiting for instructions from the officials. There had already been word that people had died. Remarkably, the authorities were determined to carry on with the game. After the dead and injured had been moved, it was then left to mounted police to clear the pitch of spectators. It would have been better for them just to get the referee to call the game off.

The game ended in a goalless draw, the players just going through the motions. Players of both sides walked dejectedly off the pitch. The result did not matter. Stoke were out of the FA Cup. Bolton lost the subsequent semi-final to Charlton. Again, that result did not matter either.

A public inquiry into the Burnden Park disaster was held but it made little difference, aside from a recognition of the immediate need to strengthen crowd barriers. Recommendations to install efficient turnstiles to count crowd numbers, making high-profile domestic league and cup games ticket-only, were wilfully ignored by many clubs, those with scant disregard for players and fans alike.

Against such a background illustrating bleak complacency, the FA and Football League enthusiastically sanctioned a post-war return to normality. It was back to the 1920s, let alone the 1940s. The Football League season for 1946/47 went ahead. Stadiums suffering bomb damage during the war were repaired but not modernised.

Bert looked forward to a new season as a married man. Army life had ended for him, being demobbed on 25 November 1945. Bert had proposed to his girlfriend Renee Day and they were married at St Nicholas' Church in the parish of Borstal in Rochester, Kent on Monday, 28 January 1946. Married life began on Abbey Road in Bert's hometown of Sandbach. Frank Swift, the Manchester City and England goalkeeper, went along to the wedding as best man. The happy couple agreed that 'Swifty' was ideal. He backed his mate up enough times on the football pitch with Manchester City and did much the same during their army days.

Both players were optimistic going into a new season. Manchester City began their quest for promotion in the 1946/47 season at Filbert Street, enjoying a comfortable 3-0 away win over Leicester City. A strong start to the season peaked with a thumping victory over Bradford Park Avenue. There was also rare controversy, at least football wise, for Bert. Manchester City won 7-2, Bert scored a penalty but he was left puzzled by the antics of an opponent after taking the spot kick.

Jackie Gibbons, a former Spurs, Brentford and England international striker, was incensed with the decision to award the penalty. He kept protesting to the referee, even as Sproston began to celebrate his goal. Gibbons had been known as one of the most gentlemanly of players. Fair to mention that his reputation took a bit of a dent. In those days match officials preferred to keep players on the pitch. Gibbons annoyed the referee so much he was told to go back to the dressing room. The game resumed without him.

The victory meant that Manchester City moved into the automatic promotion places behind Barnsley. More than 55,000 fans turned up the following week for another return to White Hart Lane for Bert – a remarkable crowd for a second division game even by the standards of the day. They trudged home after witnessing a goalless draw.

Bert enjoyed another goalscoring bonus with a penalty against Swansea Town at Maine Road. Much to his frustration, Swansea proved to be stubborn opposition. Securing promotion meant there was going to be challenging work ahead. His mate, Frank Swift, ensured that Manchester City held on for a 1-1 draw. The *Manchester Evening News* noted that Sproston's form for Manchester City over the years more than repaid the £10,000 the club paid to Spurs. It conveniently forgot that the transfer went through almost a decade earlier. There was also a seven-year suspension of league football thanks to the war.

The assessment no doubt flattered him. But he had an eye for the future. Just how to stay in football once his dodgy ligaments finally gave way? As the season progressed, one matter puzzled Bert. Just where was the next generation of footballers coming from? Players in their late teens at the outbreak of war began to make an impact, not least Stoke City defender Neil Franklin. He had seen off Stan Cullis to become an automatic choice for England. But those younger than him?

Sproston among others feared that they might be lost to football. He was able to play football as a man to boost morale.

For boys just wanting to build up their footballing skills, it was another matter.

County FAs have been dismissed by some commentators as worthless organisations, especially in the modern era of football. But in the aftermath of the Second World War, they played a prominent role in restoring the sport to full health. Cheshire FA set up a scheme to coach boys in schools and youth organisations. Just before Christmas 1946, it appointed the Crewe Alexandra manager, Frank Hill, as the chief coach.

Bert and Frank Swift joined him from Manchester City. Training sessions were limited, so too games for City's first team. One of the severest winters in decades left pitches covered in drifts of snow. Just five-a-side knockabouts in the gym were at times possible. Postponements left the Football League programme in disarray.

There was no option for midweek games, they were banned. Post-war Britain's recovery still meant austerity measures. Rationing remained in place. Give the public the bonus of watching midweek football? No. It meant an unplanned extension to the league season, lasting until June.

After a few postponements, Sproston, Swift and company welcomed the thaw in spring at the top of the second division. On 22 March 1947, they arrived at Highfield Road in Coventry looking forward to a comfortable victory. As Bert walked through the players' entrance, a Coventry City official gave him a tap on the shoulder. He had a telegram which informed him that his wife Renee had given birth to a son, Richard.

It was, of course, a fine fillip ahead of a game against a side that lost 5-1 the previous week. Both Sproston and his full-back partner Sam Barkas played well in defence. The *Coventry Evening Telegraph* commented, 'In fiddling with the ball near goal, searching for the still better position, the [Coventry] City forwards had about as much chance of retaining the ball against backs of the stamp of Barkas and Sproston as would a juggler being charged by a bull.'

Unfortunately for Bert and his mates, Coventry took a surprise lead from a rare chance on goal. Alec Herd grabbed the equaliser. Manchester City's relieved players left the field to toast the birth of Bert Sproston's baby boy, more mundanely still top of the second division table. Most football writers believed that both Manchester City and Burnley seemed destined for promotion to the first division, the equivalent of the Premier League. They were right.

The clubs met for a match billed as a title decider on 10 May 1947 at Maine Road. The match attracted a crowd of 67,672 – still a record for a second-tier league game in English football. Even so, Manchester City lost their goalkeeper for the game. Frank Swift was called up for what was being billed as the 'game of the century' – Great Britain versus the Rest of Europe at Hampden Park in Glasgow.

Not even England versus the Rest of Europe in October 1938 enjoyed such a hyperbolic billing. Those trying to promote the match thought it might help to promote peace and understanding. War broke out instead. It did give a chance for a refugee to escape from Berlin, not that anyone noticed at the time apart from his sponsor, Bert Sproston.

GB versus the Rest of Europe in May 1947 celebrated the end of the war in Europe, indeed worldwide. The gate money from a crowd of more than 135,000 went to football's world governing body, FIFA. The FA and SFA had just re-joined.

Unfortunately, the game was dubbed the 'flop of the century' – an easy 6-1 victory for the British. Much attention focused on drama off the pitch – Stanley Matthews's transfer from Stoke City to Blackpool. Bert's mate left his hometown club with just a few weeks of an extended season remaining. Stoke City narrowly missed out on winning the league championship. Matthews's former team-mates blamed him for walking out on them. Embittered Stoke fans thought the same.

The battle for promotion to the first division was a lot less controversial. Manchester City's 1-0 victory over Burnley ensured promotion. They celebrated winning the second division title at their final game of the season against Newport County on 14 June 1947 at Maine Road. City won 5-1 with George Smith scoring all five City goals. Newport were relegated along with south Wales rivals Swansea.

Once his team's celebrations began to finish, Bert went to his pigeonhole to collect his latest letters and telegrams. At least one of those telegrams gave him a smile. It was a congratulatory telegram from a young man named Ralph Freeman – the teenager then called Rolf Friedland he met in Berlin on the fateful day of 14 May 1938.

Was Bert still good enough for first division football at the grand old age of 32? Matthews was the same age but a freak. Bert, despite his injury niggles, won a vote of confidence. But oddly the manager, Sam Cowan, lost his vote of confidence despite leading his club to promotion. Manchester City's board met a few days after the club won promotion to decide the fate of the club's players.

Cowan wanted to continue combining his work as Manchester City manager with running a sports physiotherapy business in Brighton. Wilf Wild, the old-fashioned club secretary/manager, returned as caretaker manager while seeking to replace Cowan. The idea of combining sports physiotherapy with a coaching role appealed to Sproston. Meantime, Wild was quite happy to hand Sproston the captaincy.

His tenure was brief but it included the most eagerly anticipated game in Manchester since the war. More than 10,000 fans gathered outside Maine Road for more than three hours before kick-off, many without tickets. Just a few kids were lucky enough to join the 78,000 crowd.

For the matchday programme Sproston wrote, 'Although today is a "special occasion", we are regarding it as we would any league fixture. We have heard United have a good team, but I am confident we shall play well and win.' United's Irish captain, Johnny Carey, responded, 'City and United supporters have long been waiting for this game; That goes for the players too. Of course, we're all excited. The result? Well, may the best team win, but, above all, let us have a game which will be talked about – until we meet again.'

Manchester City's captain won the toss. The excitement ended there, the match turned out to be a drab goalless draw. Eric Thornton of the *Manchester Evening News* moaned that the long-awaited Manchester derby only set fans longing for entertaining displays from pre-war days.

Bert also longed for those days just to restore his old turn of pace. Age and a catalogue of injuries were taking their toll. As those injuries mounted, he decided to quit. His final playing season turned out to be a nightmare. Time to look for an alternative career.

Everything is relative in football, not least for a man who served in war. Not least for a man cast as a political propaganda tool, only to come up with his own tale of redemption in rescuing a young frightened Jewish refugee. So, nightmare might be strong in describing his 1949/50 season. But it was one he would rather forget. Manchester City were once again relegated.

His season and playing career fell apart in a 7-0 thrashing at Derby County on 3 December 1949. The notorious Baseball Ground pitch was described by the *Manchester Evening News* as 'on the heavy side'. Its headline? Manchester City were hit by a 'goal storm'. The rain pouring on the Baseball Ground bog of a pitch, before, during and after the game, was just a little soft in comparison.

City's hapless goalkeeper was Bert Trautmann, a former Nazi paratrooper and member of the Hitler Youth. After serving as a prisoner of war, Trautmann successfully morphed into a Manchester City hero. He famously played on despite being badly injured in the 1956 FA Cup Final against Birmingham City. After the game, doctors discovered that he had broken his neck. The Mancunians won the Cup.

Trautmann's skills as a goalkeeper were doubted in his early years for his club. The *Derby Evening Telegraph* reported in the game against Derby County, 'German born goalkeeper Trautmann will want to get the nightmare experience of this game, and on the form he showed he is a long, long way behind the former City and England goalkeeper Frank Swift.' For Swifty's mate Sproston the game was definitely a nightmare. Trautmann suffered from a lack of defensive cover as Sproston hobbled along thanks to a thigh injury. He struggled to carry on. No goalscoring heroics as he carried an injury against his old club Spurs before the war. City fans hoped he might make an immediate comeback. It failed to materialise.

The busy Christmas period went by with Manchester City's international full-back absent. They continued to struggle. Hopes of avoiding relegation were raised by Sproston's return against Newcastle United. 'Sproston strengthens City side,' heralded the

Manchester Evening News. The game on 21 January 1950, a 1-1 draw, made matters worse.

Fans leaving St James' Park dismissed the game as tedious. More significantly, Bert suffered his career-ending injury just ten minutes before half-time. A mistimed tackle contributed to the injury. He challenged a Newcastle player at an awkward angle, then lay on the ground wrenching himself in agony. His pre-existing problems hardly helped. Sproston lay on the stretcher determined to carry on. He felt he had suffered worse. The stretcher crew carried him off the field. 'I onner givin' up,' he told himself. This time he was unable to return to the pitch and it was for good.

The doctors diagnosed that he suffered badly torn ligaments, ordering him to rest at home in Sandbach. The Manchester City trainer, Laurie Barnett, popped in to see him regularly but nothing more than a chat over a pot of tea and biscuits seemed to take place. 'I know, I know,' fretted the injured player. 'Rest is the best cure.'

Bert's future career in football as a trainer more than likely featured in their fireside chats. A year earlier, Manchester City's then manager, Jock Thomson, sent Bert on a sports masseuse course. It was part of the FA's vocational training scheme. Thomson worked with local education authorities to set up courses in a variety of prospective careers for retired professional footballers. Future Liverpool manager, Joe Fagan, joined his team-mate Sproston on the masseuse course.

After completing his qualifications, Bert spent as much time as a patient on the masseuse couch as on the football field. After the injury at Newcastle, he did not return to Maine Road for over a month. Even then the prognosis was poor. He gave a pugnacious and optimistic response to inquiries about his fitness. 'I have been in good form when fit, and I feel certain I have many years ahead of first-class soccer.' Bert did – it just was not as a player. Manchester City limped on for the rest of the season and were relegated.

Their new manager, Les McDowall, saw no reason to keep a once valuable player. The club indicated that a transfer fee of £1,250 was required. Lancashire Combination side, Ashton, expressed an interest. So too did Stockport County; a chance to remain in the Football League. Bert rejected both offers and notified Manchester City on 27 September 1950 that he was retiring as a player. He had undergone fitness tests at Maine Road once he was put on the transfer list. He failed the lot.

Retirement rather than trying to persevere as a player in lower league football served as a matter of honour. 'No point in joining any club if I am not able to stand up to it,' he reflected. The *Manchester Evening Chronicle* broke the news to fans while describing him as 'one of the most polished backs the game has known. Sproston in later years made up in anticipation and faultless sizing up of a situation for what he lacked in speed.' Manchester City's chairman, Robert Smith, simply stated, 'He has been a grand servant.' Smith then proceeded to haggle over any pay-off owing to the grand servant.

Smith's choice of words was, to put it mildly, unfortunate. Footballers were threatening to go on strike. Being treated patronisingly as club servants hardly helped. Manchester City players grumbled over their pay, not least a cut in wages if they lost their first-team place. The dressing-room grumbles extended to rumours that Bert Sproston might miss out on accrued shares of benefit because of his long-term absence through injury. The club's attitude appeared to be, 'You're injured, tough!'

Angered by reports of growing unrest, Robert Smith told the *Manchester Evening News* that there was complete harmony at

Maine Road. Any claims to the contrary were complete nonsense. Smith moaned, 'Where's the game going? I'm not pretending to be the only little white sheep surrounded by a horde of wolves, but something will really have to be done. When players move nowadays, they want you to paint their houses, lay down new lino, install electric light fittings in the colour the wife likes best, and a hundred and one other things besides. Look what we've done for players. We've paid all benefits, whenever due, and although Bert Sproston has now left us, he's going to be given his accrued share of benefit just as if we had transferred him.'

Bert certainly did not want to be treated as a charity case. He was too proud a man to do so. He simply wanted money owed to him. There was no future at Manchester City Football Club. One final shabby episode unfolded thanks to the narcissistic nature of City's chairman. His boast of paying out benefit money accrued to Mr Sproston came with a twist.

How was Bert going to pick up his benefit cheque from the club? The answer was to dash from Stockport County's ground at Edgeley Park after working with the FA as trainer to the England amateur team. Only then would the Manchester City chairman ostentatiously present him with his cheque after the club's game with Southampton.

Bert spent more than a decade at Maine Road. He wanted to remain in football but he knew he was best off elsewhere. The hints that his time was up at Manchester City were less than subtle. To his credit, he still held the club, its players and supporters in the highest regard. Lifelong friendships were forged with players, appreciation too from fans. The following summer he took up his position as trainer at rivals Bolton Wanderers. There was to be no quiet playing retirement. There was to be joy, laughter and tears.

BOLTON'S SPONGE MAN

FOOTBALLERS WITH talent often feel little love for the game, just a way of making money. I have met them, an utterly depressing experience for any sports fan. No danger of Bert Sproston falling into such a mercenary category. Along with his brothers, he grew up living and breathing football. No wonder too that he was able to build a rapport with a football-mad German refugee. Sport allowed an escape, both metaphorically and literally.

It naturally followed that an army physical training instructor might end up as a football coach, even more so given he was a former international. The war meant an early playing retirement for some professional footballers taking the king's shilling. They took up offers of coaching and managing football clubs – young men in a hurry.

Bert's friend Matt Busby was an obvious example at Manchester United, arguably too Busby's great rival, Stan Cullis, of Wolverhampton Wanderers. The man unwittingly responsible for one of the greatest myths in English football – count me out of the Nazi salute. He was not even selected to play on that occasion.

Bert preferred to pursue his playing career, despite the intervening war years meaning veteran status. He did dabble in coaching, an unfair assessment given the importance of his work. All the while as he enjoyed his final days at Manchester City, the

Cheshire FA tapped up Sproston for his services. They were keen to prevent a generation of players being lost to the game.

Unless they were signed up by league clubs before the outbreak of war, their chances of making it in the professional game were limited. It was time to help the teenagers looking to pursue a career in professional football. A veteran, but still a relatively young man, Bert wanted to remain in football. He did not want to run a pub or, more realistically, rejoin the Sproston family building firm. Then again, he did list his hobby as carpentry in Manchester City's programme notes.

Bolton Wanderers made it known that they were keen to modernise their backroom team. On Friday, 6 July 1951 they appointed former international footballer Bert Sproston as the club's trainer and qualified sports masseuse. According to the *Manchester Evening News*, the appointment was part of a desire to implement a modernisation programme along the 'luxury lines' of the Arsenal dressing room. Quite how Arsenal were held in such high regard, aside from being serially successful, was not made clear.

Bolton's manager Bill Ridding knew that English football needed to evolve. Innovative ideas were required, perhaps old ideas ignored by the establishment. His playing staff needed the best possible support to enjoy success. Ridding identified Sproston as a thoughtful and potentially inspirational addition to his back-room staff. He would not just be a sponge man to look after aches, sprains and pains. Of course, his qualifications as a sports masseuse mattered but so too did his immense knowledge of football.

Even as a shy young player, Bert occasionally offered his views on the game. His views on how the game of football ought to be played have been outlined earlier but they are worth delving into more deeply. Sproston's football philosophy was simple but effective:

- Defenders need to be constructive as well as destructive
- Conquering the art of positional play – no player can go far in the game without it
- Value every position on the field, defender or striker
- Coaches need to ensure young players are ready both mentally and physically
- Maintaining discipline and fitness including cutting out alcohol and smoking
- Be flexible, forget rigid tactics and enjoy the game.

These views were all articulated before the war as a young player. They were quite possibly views formulated around the Sproston tea table in Sandbach among a committed sporting family.

As a disciple of the defensive arts of football, there was the zeal of the convert. International ambition first motivated him to go into print. His rivalry with George Male of Arsenal was documented earlier. Bert needed to clarify his own opinions and to do so in a syndicated newspaper column by-lined as Bert Sproston, Leeds United's famous full-back. 'Discussions about the most difficult position to fill on the football field are very popular among football players and followers, and cause many hours of amusement,' he wrote. 'Seldom do they lead to any definite decision because in the case of every position it is possible to prove that it is the most exacting one of all.'

Sproston elaborated further on the merits of the art of defending. 'My intention in raising the question was not, however, to discuss the merits of full-back as opposed to forwards. Much more important is the realisation that full-back play is just as much a science as forward or half-back play. Perhaps a different kind of science, but still a science in every sense of the word. It is not just a question of tackling fiercely and kicking hard.'

Just one overarching principle for decent full-back play to be articulated. He wrote, 'A good hefty "blind" kick will certainly clear the lines, but that of course, is not the only consideration. Occasions do arise, of course, in times of undue stress and so on, when the full-back might be excused for worrying only about relieving the pressure on his goal. In normal circumstances, however, he should try to be constructive as well as destructive; to help his own attackers by the use of long accurate passes rather than wild kicks. That perhaps is the hallmark of a good full-back.'

Not just the full-backs but all defenders needed to employ constructive tactics, including goalkeepers. A ball-playing goalkeeper is considered a 21st-century concept. Bert advocated such attributes in the 1930s, no doubt influenced by his friend and team-mate, Frank Swift. 'The goalkeeper too should come into the defensive organisation,' Sproston argued. 'No need for him to stand between the posts waiting to be shot at. Let him be an extra defender in every way, helping his colleagues out of trouble in many ways – by advancing from his goal, running out to take centres from the wing, being ready for the quick back pass, and so on.'

His version of playing out from the back was ahead of its time. But there was the insurance policy of goalkeepers being allowed to pick up back passes. Lev Yashin, Gordon Banks and Pat Jennings all played in goal with exemplary distribution in post-war years. Quite whether they read the Bolton Wanderers trainer's advice is doubtful. It does though bear testament to the adage of there's nothing new in sport.

Given his own travails in breaking through as a professional footballer, it is no surprise he took a keen interest in the welfare of young talent. Saturday afternoons turning out for Sandbach Ramblers in the Cheshire County League and rejection by Huddersfield Town kept him grounded. Sproston reflected in February 1938, 'The story of football, even in my comparatively short association with the first-class game, abounds in cases of players who have gone up with a flare, like a rocket, and equally have come down flop, like the stick.'

Who is to blame? Managers, fans and the press all put too much pressure on a player, who might be good, but hardly a world beater. An established player is subject to criticism, fairly or otherwise. But an unknown performer, a kid just starting out, is not treated with 'such deadly seriousness as the established star'. It was easier, Sproston argued, for the young rising star to make a show and get the good press. 'He has begun to make a reputation, but has to consistently prove himself a real footballer, week after week. Not everybody is capable of doing so, very few.'

Most athletes owe a debt of gratitude to their parents and Bert was no different. His mother sternly oversaw that all was above board in his transfer dealings and his father was influential in his early career, who as the stalwart of Sandbach Ramblers FC and Sandbach Cricket Club, demanded caution in developing young talent, not least his own sons.

'I have no doubt in my own mind that many young players fail to make good because they are advanced before they are ready for it, either physically or mentally,' Sproston asserted. 'When I went to Leeds as a professional footballer – at 18 years of age – my father made a stipulation that even if I were considered good enough, I wasn't to be pushed up into the first team for a year, or two years for preference. My father knew of the danger of my playing regularly in the first team before I had thoroughly developed physically, many players are "broken" by the strenuous nature of league football before they have fully developed.'

John Sproston must have been a formidable man to dictate to a Football League club just how they might treat his son. There may be question marks about how young players are treated now. It might be a relief for youth coaches to come across a parent cautioning against giving their son too much first-team exposure. Mr Sproston never played sport at first-class level, as his son Bert might acknowledge. He was certainly well versed in sport and confident enough to offer advice to all his sons, whether football or cricket.

Bert wrote, 'The young player who makes good is the one who can keep praise in its proper place and appreciate it at its true worth. This game of football is one in which a player can always be learning something; by watching others; by paying due attention to the things which are told him by those who know. The player whose head swells to such an extent that his ears are closed to advice doesn't make the progress in the game which he should make.'

Just what of the fundamental structure of the game? England and the rest of the home nations ignored the World Cup. Europe's leading teams pushed England close on their visits to London, especially Austria and Italy in the infamous 'Battle of Highbury'. As for Germany, they were not a top-ranked nation. Even so, one sidebar to Bert Sproston's missive on youth football read, 'The international soccer match between Germany and England to be played on May 14 in Berlin seems to be as popular in Germany as the FA Cup Final is in England. The Olympic Stadium, Berlin, can accommodate 100,000 people, yet 470,000 applications for tickets have been received.'

Bolton's latest recruit's experience of continental football was limited. It hardly made him alone in English football. But even before embarking for Germany on the infamous European tour of spring 1938, he offered forthright views of how to play the game. He recognised that English football favoured a rigid system. The 'continentals' were far more flexible, not least the world champions Italy, their great rivals, the *Wunderteam* of Austria, even Germany under the guidance of Sepp Herberger.

Another syndicated column highlighted the 'art' of positional play. It was filed for the new year editions of 1938 and was yet another early insight into his football philosophy. Schoolboy textbooks gave the rigid positions for association football. They did the same for rugby union football, and while rugby tactics may have evolved the positions remain. Not the case in soccer, not even technically, at times, for Bert's favoured position of right-back.

Back in the 1930s, Sproston commented, 'Before a football match starts it is the custom for the players of the two teams to "line up" in the position which they occupy – the back, half-back and forwards neatly arranged on the field of play. It is safe to say that never, while play is in progress, would it be found that the eleven members of a side were even approximately in those places on the field of play which they occupied before the match started.' Players hardly bothered 'to keep the positions in which the programme says they are playing'.

It seems a statement of the obvious but Bert felt the need to point it out to the average British supporter. There was no need for fans of European club or international football given they were quite used to flexible styles of play. But even the FA may well have noted a trend in British football to follow the European example.

One of the reasons put forward for numbering players' shirts just happened to be that it was easier for spectators to identify them. A player's position printed in the programme was no longer of any use. Numbers were more useful. Hence, the FA at its summer 1938 meeting in Scarborough introduced the innovation of numbering players' shirts. As mentioned earlier, the innovation began badly. The England right-back Bert Sproston still caused confusion, wearing a different number than the one published in the programme for the game against Wales. The British fan's habit of scribbling in names and numbers had begun. It only effectively ended with the adoption of squad numbers.

Bert found it a remarkable fact that players failed to stay in position given that a keen sense of positional play is essential for any footballer. Did British footballers of the 1930s fail to grasp the importance of positional play? Not necessarily so according to the young England full-back, 'Positional play does not mean keeping in position; it means the art of being in the right position at the right time. These are two very different things. It would be possible for example, to say that a right full-back was in the correct position, even though he were on the left side of the field. He would be out of position, but if the needs of the moment made it advisable for his to go over to the other side of the field, he could be praised for clever positioning.'

He went on to suggest that the position attributed to the footballer in an English matchday programme of the era just happened to be irrelevant. 'A player can be out of position, according to the programme, but still be in the right place at the right time,' Sproston wrote.

In a sense, Bert sought to justify his own style of play. His speed and powers of recovery drew praise from admirers. Finding himself out of position in the first place was noted by his critics. It was a feature of assessments of his play even in wartime matches. Millwall did put him in as their makeshift striker in the number 9 shirt for the benefit of their fans to avoid any confusion.

Bert wrote, 'Without conquering the art of positional play no player can hope to go very far in the game. It is a secret of success in any football.' He then acknowledged his own bias. His manager at Leeds, Billy Hampson, presumably agreed with him. 'Perhaps my view is distorted because of my own job as a defender, but I would say that for no one is positional play more important than for a full back,' he continued. 'Of this I am quite certain. The most important.'

Certainly, employing a former international to look after aches and pains as well as tactical advice made sense. His valuable experience as a physical training instructor also helped. Most clubs, not just Arsenal, employed ex-professional footballers in the role. A couple of Wembley appearances provided career highs as a member of the Bolton backroom staff.

Bert felt frustrated back in 1953 as Bolton's trainer. His old friend Stanley Matthews had cemented his place as a national icon by helping Blackpool to win the FA Cup. Matthews's team beat Bolton 4-3, Stanley Mortensen scoring a hat-trick. But the game still became known as the 'Matthews final'.

There was plenty of sentiment for Bert's old England room-mate off the pitch but there was none in a fiercely contested game. Bolton's trainer was on the pitch after just a couple of minutes played. Sproston spent the break frantically attending to Eric Bell, Bolton's playmaker. He limped through the rest of the game, somehow managing to put Bolton 3-1 up. Sproston also ran relays from the bench and on to the pitch to attend Lofthouse. The Press Association reporter noted, 'The Bolton trainer, Bert Sproston, had been a very busy man all through [the game].'

For all the talk of the romance of the Matthews final, it was a dirty game. The referee allowed plenty of time beyond the 90 minutes because there were so many breaks for injuries. It went into football folklore, partly because of Matthews, mainly because of the craze for television sets ahead of Queen Elizabeth's coronation. The 1953 FA Cup Final was the first transmitted to a mass TV audience. Bert, as he constantly ran on to the pitch, never appeared as much on TV, before or since. Not even in the hard-fought 1958 cup final.

Blackpool fought back to score a last-minute winner to send their fans and much of the country wild. Matthews helped to set up the goal for Bill Perry. He was the man of the moment, again. As a reward for Blackpool's players, the club gave them each a present of a cigarette lighter. Matthews never received one. It would not surprise his old mate Bert as Matthews shared his disdain for the habit. 'Hardly the ideal presentation gift for a professional footballer,' Matthews commented. Sproston agreed.

He returned home with his battered and bruised players. Another chance to lift the FA Cup came along. Bolton returned to Wembley five years later hoping to make amends, ruin another romantic script. It was a professional duty. Personally, it was difficult. A challenge to supress emotions, just pure football.

MUNICH 1958

A FREEZE once again sets in over the country. A light dusting of snow lies across an array of football fields. A football fan walked towards one of the pitches, drooped into his overcoat with his shoulders hunched as he tried to combat the cold. A shrill whistle rings out, similar to one blown by a station porter. The fan pauses and smiles. The man in charge of the workout is bringing back memories.

Bert Sproston tried to control his group of players in the practice match. They respected him, even feared him, but for once they took no notice of him. Instead, the players focused on the smartly-dressed stranger approaching their trainer, affectionately known as the 'sponge man'. He was the players' physio, also a coach with a wealth of playing experience.

Few fans watched their sessions, especially in freezing conditions. They looked at their visitor, feeling just a little mystified. Bert embraced the stranger. So just who was the dapper gentleman? Maybe he was a businessman invited on to the club's board? Just another nosey journalist? No, there was a far more poignant reason. Little did they know that the blast of a whistle once signalled the departure of a train taking the stranger away from danger and into freedom. An old friend just wanted to be reunited with the former England international footballer. He simply wanted to console him.

Bert needed friends at a time of grief for so many in football. He had just lost one of his best friends. Ralph Freeman, once known to Bert as Rolf Friedland, understood the mourning process. He understood those consumed by tragedy, those grieving in deep personal loss. A loss shared by a nation in shock. Every one of the Bolton Wanderers players and staff remembered the events unfolding on the afternoon of Thursday, 6 December 1958. They did so for the rest of their lives. They mourned for a rival football club, Manchester United. So too did the rest of the football world.

Bert and his wife Renee settled down that fateful day in front of the television. He had arrived home early. Bolton's officials had already alerted him to grim news coming out of Munich concerning their neighbours, Manchester United. Bert did not expect confirmation of the tragedy to come at the beginning of BBC *Children's Hour*.

The newsreader, Richard Baker, was almost apologetic. He read the news report as follows, 'And the reason you've come over to the news studio is that we have to report a serious air crash at Munich Airport. We haven't full details yet, but the aircraft that has crashed is an Elizabethan. It was on charter from British European Airways and travelling from Belgrade to Manchester. The crash was at Munich Airport. On board was the Manchester United football team returning from the World [European] Cup match in Yugoslavia. With them were sports writers of Fleet Street newspapers and, as far as we know, team officials. Twenty-five of the passengers and crew are believed to have died.'

The charter plane was due to arrive at Ringway Airport in Cheshire (Manchester Airport) at 5pm. There was no sign of the aircraft. Airport staff had already huddled worried relatives into an anteroom to brief them. Word of a tragedy quickly spread across the Greater Manchester area.

Once again in his lifetime, the anguish resulting from a sports-related event made him feel numb. More so than anything before, certainly far more than the behaviour of England's football team just before the war. Bert needed to know more from Munich, desperate for reassurance.

Darkness descended on a bleak February evening. The Sprostons cooked some tea but their appetite had unsurprisingly disappeared. They were consumed by stress. Renee tried to contact her friends, especially Doris, the wife of Manchester City's former goalkeeper, Frank Swift. Tears flowed. Swifty was the best man at their wedding. They knew so many others on board the fateful flight.

Radio news remained in the 1950s an appointment to listen. Bert and Renee sat down to listen intently to the BBC Radio *Six O'Clock News* on the BBC Home Service. It gave further details of the British European Airways Airspeed AS 57 Ambassador (Elizabethan) aircraft, flight BEA 609, that had crashed at Munich-Riem airport. It had gone into a fatal skid on its third attempt to lift off from a runway that was covered in slush and ice.

On board, the BBC once again reported, were Manchester United's team, club officials and journalists. It was meant to be their triumphant return from United's European Cup quarter-final victory the previous afternoon against Red Star Belgrade. The victims of the tragedy included some of the cream of British and Irish football. Former England and Manchester City goalkeeper Frank Swift was travelling back from Belgrade via Munich as a journalist for the *News of the World* newspaper.

The BBC bulletin mentioned the names of survivors. The name Frank Swift was not among them. The horrible realisation dawned on the loving couple. Swifty was dead. Mixed emotions overcame them. Did he reboard the plane at Munich? How was Doris, his wife? Besides Swifty, too many old friends had been lost in the tragedy or fighting for their lives.

For Bert and Renee, as with so many across the country, it was a baffling tragedy. For them a personal tragedy, the loss of a dear friend, so many other friends. Not just a tragedy for Manchester United fans, but all fans of the national game of football. There was genuine shock, not just from supporters of Manchester United, any football club. The entire country mourned.

On the following morning, it was confirmed that 21 people had died in the crash. These included seven Manchester United players – Roger Byrne, Geoff Bent, Mark Jones, Billy Whelan, Eddie Colman, Tommie Taylor and David Pegg. Some days later Duncan Edwards, a stellar talent, died from his injuries in hospital, despite desperate efforts from German doctors to save him – eight Manchester United players dead.

The German government inquiry later concluded that ice on the aircraft wings may have been a factor. It built up as the plane ferried back and forth from the terminal building. No blame was apportioned but the plane ought to have stayed in Munich until the weather cleared. Any speculation that the pilots were too anxious to return home was discounted.

It concluded, 'During the stop of almost two hours at Munich, a rough layer of ice formed on the upper surface of the wings as a result of snowfall. This layer of ice considerably impaired the aerodynamic efficiency of the aircraft, had a detrimental effect on the acceleration of the aircraft during the take-off process and increased the required unstick-speed. Thus, under the conditions obtaining at the time of take-off, the aircraft was not able to attain this speed within the rolling distance available. The decisive cause of the accident lay in this. It is not out of the question that, in the final phase of the take-off process, further causes may also have had an effect on the accident.'

Rescue teams brought Frank Swift out of the wreckage alive. Sadly, he died in hospital just hours later. The former Manchester City and England goalkeeper had no need to go to the game in Belgrade. His *News of the World* match reports were confined to Saturday afternoon games for the biggest-selling Sunday newspaper but he was dedicated to his new job. He wanted to assess in person the Manchester United squad, the so-called 'Busby Babes', as they attempted to win the European Cup, earn recognition as the world's finest club side. He wanted to gain a further insight into the managerial genius of his old friend, Matt Busby. Also, United faced a potential championship decider in a game against Wolverhampton Wanderers the following weekend. It was ideal preparation to join them on the trip to Belgrade.

Another international goalkeeper remembered Swifty's last moments. Harry Gregg was later heralded as a hero of the Munich disaster. The United goalie survived the crash but went back into the mangled wreckage to help rescue fellow passengers. He did so despite the risk of an explosion from leaking fuel. Those he rescued included Vera Lukic, the wife of a Yugoslav diplomat and her 22-month-old baby daughter, Venona. Mrs Lukic suffered critical injuries but survived along with her daughter.

Sitting up in hospital, Gregg talked to waiting journalists through the final moments before the crash. Frank Swift was in good spirits, living up to his reputation as a dressing-room jester during his playing days. He remembered Frank Swift standing at the back of the aircraft fatefully saying, 'This is the last flight you'll make, lads.' On the third attempt to lift off some of the passengers feared that the flight was doomed. They had a premonition. Memories of Swift's dark words remained in the struggling minds of survivors.

Gregg sat towards the front of the aircraft. He was lucky. Much of the damage was at the rear of the plane. 'He [the pilot] started to brake, but could not stay on the runway,' Gregg said. 'The plane ran along the ground, got into some marshy ground, and just broke up. The rear part came away and hit some sort of shack. It broke into flames at once.'

Along with Frank Swift, seven others working as journalists died in the crash. Henry Rose was among them, the *Daily Express* correspondent, who sat in Berlin's Olympiastadion back in May 1938 and condemned the Nazi salute made by England's footballers. The newspaper's owner, Lord Beaverbrook, supported appeasement and backed the players' futile gesture. Rose thought differently and was allowed to express his view. The *Daily Express* in tribute commented, 'He was a fearless writer. He was at times outrageously frank.'

Bert knew many of the other victims and survivors, not least the Manchester United manager. Matt Busby was Bert's captain in his final international game of football, Great Britain's wartime match against Belgium. A Roman Catholic priest gave Busby the sacrament of the sick, commonly known as the 'last rites', as he lay in an oxygen tent fighting for his life. His wife, Jean, along with his son, Sandy, and daughter, Sheena, were at his bedside in Munich. Prayers were offered at their home Catholic parish church of St Alphonsus near to the Old Trafford football ground. Busby survived.

Bert and Matt were once rivals on the pitch, Busby playing for Manchester City before Sproston joined the club. Both became garrisoned at Aldershot at the outset of war and became friends playing together in army representative games throughout the conflict. Neither knew as the nation came to terms with the Munich air disaster that they would soon be reunited at a Wembley cup final.

As Matt Busby recovered in a Munich hospital, the grim task of repatriating bodies back to England began. Within days, funerals were held across the Greater Manchester area, thousands attending them. Liam Whelan's funeral took place in Dublin, the pope sending a message of condolence to his family. Manchester United reserve team players travelled to Doncaster for the funeral of David Pegg.

The funeral of Frank Swift was held on Wednesday, 12 February 1958 at St Margaret's Church, Whalley Range, Manchester. Bert was one of the pall-bearers. He was joined in carrying Frank's coffin by other Manchester City team-mates of a much-loved player. They were Les McDowall, Laurie Barnett, Fred Tilson, Eric Brook and Eric Westwood. Scores of mourners held a vigil outside the packed church.

On the eve of the funeral, his successor as Manchester City's goalkeeper, Bert Trautmann, told the *Manchester Evening News* that it was a very sad moment for him and every other player at the club. He wrote, 'At this moment we are thinking mostly of the relatives of those who have been lost. For we must not consider only the loss football has sustained. I think that first and foremost we should keep those relatives in our hearts. No one can even reasonably estimate the loss they have suffered though their memories should live on.'

Friends of the victims needed comforting too. Hence, Ralph Freeman's decision to go to Bolton to be reunited with his friend,

Bert Sproston. As a football-mad teenager in Berlin, he knew of the legendary stories of Frank Swift. Not least, he learned from Bert that it was quite fine to tease big Swifty with the tale of the 1934 FA Cup Final. Manchester City lost the previous year's final to Everton. Swift's team returned to Wembley to beat Portsmouth 2-1, the Pompey goal coming as the result of a mistake by Swift. His goal remained intact for the rest of the game. Such was his frazzled state, he fainted and collapsed on to the pitch at the final whistle.

Ralph's son Alan reflected on the importance of the bond between his father and Sproston at a time of immense stress. His dad struggled but succeeded in setting up a children's charity. Ralph was inspired by the humanity of an English footballer, who rescued him as a teenager from the Nazis. Time to pay back society, its most vulnerable members.

It was important to trek north to visit Bert. Ralph needed to offer warmth and sympathy. Tell him that he still remembered the fateful evening outside Berlin's Olympiastadion, how Bert not only gave him a chance in life but saved his life. His son Alan recalled, 'I was only five years old when that terrible plane crash happened. Having said that my father certainly referred to the crash, young lives with truly exciting potential snuffed out. There was an aura to the Busby Babes that my dad admired.'

Above all there was Duncan Edwards. German doctors tried in vain to save him. He died some days after the crash. Alan commented, 'He [Ralph, Alan's dad] talked about his admiration for Duncan Edwards. Perhaps due to the goal he scored in the 1956 friendly against West Germany. Any victory over Germany resonated strongly with him but this particular victory must have had a particularly sweet taste to it as it coincided with his 36th birthday, 26 May 1956.'

The game marked the return of an England football team to Berlin's Olympiastadion. More than 4,000 England fans, most of them British servicemen stationed in Germany, cheered on their heroes. England beat West Germany 3-1. Edwards evaded a series of tackles as he stormed forward to thump the ball into the bottom corner of the net for England's opening goal. The Pathé News commentator told British cinema-goers, 'It did much to restore England's waning soccer prestige in Europe.'

It was also another victory over the world champions. A couple of years earlier, Ralph joined Bert at Wembley as England again beat West Germany 3-1. Only one player from the ill-fated match of 14 May 1938 in Berlin turned out: England's remarkable evergreen legend, Stanley Matthews. Herberger described the wizard of dribble's performance as phenomenal. *Die Welt* remarked, 'The truth is that England has ceased to be a football power. Her only strength is the phenomenal Stanley Matthews.' Matthews left Wembley on 1 December 1954 with his reputation even further enhanced.

Another hot day in May and another team celebrating victory. Memories of Berlin, 1938 as teams took to the field at Wembley in May 1958? Not quite. Much of England yearned for romance in sport. No dark political propaganda, no hyperbolic tributes to the status of sport in society. Most football fans, or those with little or no regard for sport, wanted Manchester United to complete a fairy tale. They urged them to overcome the physical and psychological pain of the Munich disaster, just three months earlier, to go and win the FA Cup.

Bert politely disagreed. It was his job to help Bolton Wanderers teach the fabled Busy Babes, the Red Devils, a harsh sporting lesson. To be blunt, he thought that Bolton possessed better players than United's patched-up team, and it proved to be the case. Bolton beat Manchester United 2-0, a triumph to remember, albeit in pained and emotional circumstances for their defeated opponents.

Celebrations appeared a little muted, unusually polite. Bolton's captain Nat Lofthouse led his team up Wembley's 39 steps to the royal box to receive the trophy. He shook hands with the Duke of Edinburgh, then lifted the FA Cup in the direction of his cheering fans.

Once the players received their medals and walked down back to the pitch, they began to head straight for the dressing rooms. Nobody was in the mood for the traditional celebrations. It was left to Bert to gather them together and send them on their way around Wembley on a victory lap. 'You must do the lap of honour. It will be the biggest thing in your career and you will remember it for all your life,' he told them.

Bolton's Roy Hartle recalled, 'He [Sproston] was right as it turned out, but at the time we just couldn't see what all the fuss was about. After Munich, the match was a bit meaningless I suppose.' Instinctively, Bert made the right decision, gathering his players and insisting they enjoyed their moment of glory.

One other man understood. As Bolton's players celebrated beneath Wembley's twin towers, Bert heard a knock on the dressing-room door. A familiar figure stood outside propped up by a walking stick, still a fearsome figure to most people in football despite his injuries. Not so to his old friend Bert, nor to the Bolton manager, Bill Ridding. They let him in.

In the build-up to the match, Ridding played up the potential role of Bolton as party poopers in the national press, constantly telling journalists that they were merely the FA Cup Final's 'other team'. Sproston egged him on but it was a time for magnanimity in victory. Matt Busby allowed his assistant Jimmy Murphy to lead out his Manchester United side for the FA Cup Final but he felt it incumbent on him to congratulate his rivals from down the road in Bolton.

Busby told them, 'Congratulations. I want you to know I think the better team won. There's no doubt about it.' Ridding broke into tears. Bert stood beside him impassively. Ridding said, 'Thank you Matt. All I can say is that there's more in life than one victory. We can't tell you how much it means to be seeing you here.' Given the circumstances, it was remarkable that Manchester United had even made the final.

Bert then signalled to Nat Lofthouse, scorer of both Bolton goals, to come out of the bath and don a towel. It was a minor miracle that Lofthouse played. Bert carried him off the pitch at White Hart Lane some weeks earlier in a defeat to Tottenham. He struggled as the trainer, with a little more sophistication than using a bucket and trusty magic sponge, to restore Lofthouse to fitness in time for the cup final at Wembley.

Lofthouse recalled of the meeting with Busby in the Wembley dressing rooms, 'Something – something very special – made this man come into our dressing room in what must have been one of the saddest moments of his career to congratulate us on beating his team. Tommy Banks summed it up for all of us when he said, after Matt had hobbled quietly away, "That's the finest sportsman you will ever see."' As Matt Clough reflected in his excellent biography of Nat Lofthouse *Lofty*, conflicting emotions meant there was a bittersweet nature to Bolton's 1958 FA Cup victory.

Spurs fan Ralph Freeman was at the FA Cup Final courtesy of a ticket from the Bolton trainer. He had hoped to meet Bert after the league game between Bolton and Spurs at White Hart Lane a few weeks earlier. No such luck as Bert took his star player to hospital. A surgically pinned shoulder meant that Bert needed to take gentle care of Lofthouse prior to the 1958 FA Cup Final and managed to restore him to fitness.

Busby congratulated Lofthouse on his goals and performance. Not only did he score twice but he was kicked all over the lush Wembley turf. The man nicknamed the 'Lion of Vienna' while impressing on international duty for England against Austria, managed to overcome the worst Manchester United's youngsters managed to throw at him.

Lofthouse's second goal against United was controversial, charging into their Irish goalkeeper, Harry Gregg, a hero of Munich. Bert, and indeed Busby, remembered continental teams' disdain for the tactic in the pre-war days. England, for example, decided against charging Germany's goalkeeper, Hans Jakob, during the infamous 1938 game in Berlin. It came as no surprise to Busby or Sproston, that Lofthouse's tactics were soon outlawed. Football, or soccer as the sport was happily nicknamed by British fans in those days, was supposed to be the beautiful game. Goalkeepers were given greater protection, a perennial source of irritation to strikers.

As much as the players needed to be cajoled by Sproston into traditional celebrations at Wembley, the subsequent festivities turned out to be a little raucous. Alcohol flowed in abundance. The party began at the Café Royal, moved to a West End nightclub mobbed by Bolton fans, and ended up at the team hotel in the early hours of Sunday morning.

The journey home to Bolton also turned out to be eventful for the victorious team. Not everyone associated with Manchester United shared the generosity and magnanimity of Matt Busby.

Youths wearing United colours in Salford pelted Bolton's open-top bus with missiles including stones, bricks and even bags of flour and rotten tomatoes. The club's trainer, Bert Sproston, was hit on the jaw by one of the projectiles. 'Suffered worse,' summed up his reaction. He commented to journalists, 'The lads are treating it as a joke.' Standing outside Bolton town hall in front of thousands of his club's celebrating fans, 'We did get a bit of a rough time through Manchester, but we are coming through again with the cup next year.'

Nat Lofthouse echoed Bert's sentiments, dismissively telling fans, 'There were a number of hooligans on the route when we were passing through Manchester. Some of the players had narrow escapes and had flour over their jackets. But don't worry, we'll come through Manchester again next year if we win the cup.'

One man was less impressed. Matt Busby wanted to forget the FA Cup Final defeat. Instead, he felt forced to comment on his club's errant fans. He said, 'It is all very disappointing. I think children might be to blame, but it certainly doesn't mirror the feelings of all true sportsmen in Manchester, and I'd like Bolton to know that.'

Munich 1958 left an indelible memory on all involved in English football. It remains a significant event for the modern game, sadly for some football fans more than misguided others. Bert mourned the loss of one of his best friends, Frank Swift – the best man at his wedding to Renee. Very few knew the sad emotions stirred by an occasion without a fairy-tale ending.

Bolton's FA Cup victory in May 1958 was one final triumph for a football man, though he served Bolton for well over a decade more. He did so, as with the rest of his football career, with pride, humanity and dignity. Sadly, to the distress of his family and friends such as Ralph, it was a cup final he struggled to remember. Just perhaps by a quirk of cruel fate, he would have been happy to forget his game for England against Germany on 14 May 1938. Not the match, just events before kick-off.

Bert loved caressing a football. The ball, itself, became a curse. He suffered from an illness induced by years of playing a beautiful but, in terms of players' long-term health, too often an ugly game.

TRUE GENTLEMEN

ONE STRAIGHTFORWARD tribute from the families of Bert Sproston and Ralph Freeman: gentlemen both. Gentlemanly conduct is an old-fashioned concept in sport. Corinthian values of sportsmanship with a competitive edge influenced Bert and Rolf's values. It went beyond sportsmanship, a simple lesson for life.

Bert's daughter-in-law, Janice Sproston, and Ralph's son, Alan Freeman, described them as models of decency and civility. It might be dismissed as family bias but they are not alone in their view. Both men lived dignified lives and, at times, demonstrated undoubted bravery.

They shared a deep love of football. Bert was the international footballer, a man of whom his family is deeply and rightly proud. A cultured but steely footballer and a respected mentor of generations following him into the game. Ralph escaped Berlin where just playing in a park kickabout was difficult. He fought in war against his Nazi tormentors. On being demobbed, he built a successful business career, then devoted his time in retirement to charity. His family too are proud of him.

Ultimately, the sport brought them together. It did so in remarkable circumstances – the staging of the most infamous game in English sporting history. For Bert, it was a matter of pride and redemption, just hours after being forced to make the Nazi salute in the cause of appeasement. Their relationship is a salutary tale of the clash of sport and politics.

Bert Sproston died on 27 January 2000 in Bolton, aged 84. For several years he suffered from an all-too-common debilitating illness for professional footballers, Alzheimer's disease. He loved sport, whether it be football or cricket. He never cared for politicians, those dabbling in sport, not after his experiences in Berlin. Sadly, his sport exacted a further price. Nothing to do with the dubious antics in Berlin but everything to do with his long-term health and welfare.

Twin evils bedevil sport. A desire to exploit athletes for commercial or political gain goes back to the birth of organised games. An ignorance, wilful or otherwise, of how to care for player welfare. Both exist in the tale of Bert Sproston and the German football refugee.

Bert Sproston's intervention, allowing a teenager to escape from the Nazis in Berlin, was an act of moral decency. Perhaps not the most famous example, but still an inspiring one. Just who can fail to be compassionate for a refugee? Especially as avenues were closing for them to find safe havens.

Modern crises demonstrate that many care little for those fleeing for their lives. Politicians can give in to their voters' base instincts. The Nazis even hypocritically challenged the leaders of democratic nations to recognise the human rights of the very people they were banishing, then murdering.

Hannah Arendt wrote in *The Origins of Totalitarianism* that the great shock European governments suffered through the arrival of refugees prior to the war was the realisation that it was, 'impossible to get rid of them or transform them into nationals of the country of refuge'. Arendt posed the question of how the refugee can be made deportable again? She offered as a conclusion, 'The notion that statelessness is primarily a Jewish problem was a pretext used by all governments who tried to settle the problem by ignoring it. None of the statesmen was aware that Hitler's solution of the Jewish problem, first to reduce the German Jews to a non-recognised minority in Germany, then to drive them as stateless people across the borders, and finally to gather them back from everywhere in order to ship them to extermination camps, was an eloquent demonstration to the rest the world how to really "liquidate" all problems concerning minorities and the stateless.'

England's right-back helped a German football fan feeling it was the right thing to do. No room for cynicism, no questioning of motive, no publicity gained either. Sadly, the Nazis were the propaganda victors in the aftermath of England's Nazi salute in May 1938. Bert Sproston's meeting with Rolf Friedland went unnoticed. Rolf was quite happy with the latter, if not the former.

Rolf understood that England's footballers were not endorsing Adolf Hitler by making the Nazi salute. It might have unsettled his young mind. Any confusion would have been cleared up in subsequent chats with Bert. There was never ever any seal of approval for Hitler and his doctrine of evil. Any suggestions to the contrary are ridiculous. These include attempts to draw comparisons with modern-day footballers' gestures, which are meant to highlight issues of racial justice.

Quite why and how can confronting racism and discriminatory behaviour become controversial? It is not a matter of being on the left or right wing of politics or stuck firmly in the centre circle. Any gesture on a sports field or podium can be interpreted as political, apolitical, or just plain neutral. Maybe a cry for help or an appeal to human decency?

England's former manager Gareth Southgate defended his players during the Euro 2020 tournament as they 'took the knee' – a gesture deemed by many as political. It was a gesture borrowed from the American football playbook by Colin Kaepernick in his campaign to highlight racial discrimination. Southgate wrote in his 'dear England' letter, 'Our players are role models. And, beyond the confines of the pitch, we must recognise the impact they can have on society. We must give them the confidence to stand up for their team-mates and the things that matter to them as people. I have never believed that we should just stick to football.

'I know my voice carries weight, not because of who I am but because of the position that I hold. At home, I'm below the kids and the dogs in the pecking order but publicly I am the England men's football team manager. I have a responsibility to the wider community to use my voice, and so do the players. It's their duty to continue to interact with the public on matters such as equality, inclusivity, and racial injustice, while using the power of their voices to help put debates on the table, raise awareness and educate.'

Nelson Mandela recognised the power of sport for good rather than as a tool for evil. Mandela declared in 2000, at the inaugural Laureus World Sports Awards in Monaco, 'Sport has the power to change the world. It has the power to inspire. It has the power to unite people in a way that little else does. It speaks to youth in a language they understand. Sport can create hope where once there was only despair. It is more powerful than governments in breaking down racial barriers. It laughs in the face of all types of discrimination.'

The Nazi mouthpiece *Völkischer Beobachter* declared on Germany winning the right to stage the 1936 Olympics, 'The next

Olympic Games will take place in Berlin. Blacks must be excluded. We demand it.' To the Nazis, Jewish lives never mattered. Arab lives never mattered. Asian lives never mattered. Slavic lives never mattered. Black lives never mattered.

England footballers of the 1930s, including Bert Sproston, were trapped in sport's curious political zoo. The English sporting establishment learned nothing from the events in Berlin's Olympiastadion on 14 May 1938. Why would they? The British government backed them. The FA boss Stanley Rous felt emboldened. He ordered England's players to make a fascist salute once again before a game with Italy in May 1939 – this time in Milan at the San Siro.

The FA's own record on racism was dubious to put it mildly. In the 1920s, Plymouth Argyle's Jack Leslie was selected to play for England. He turned up, he was black, he did not play. A decade later, Stoke City's captain Frank Soo in the never played for England. His wartime and victory international appearances served as token honours.

Most young working-class lads just did as they were told. They were professional sportsmen. Those running the FA stood accused of being amateurish. A similar criticism might be made of the political establishment. Ministers bizarrely debated in the months leading up to England's footballers' trip to Germany the merits of inviting Luftwaffe boss Hermann Göring to the Grand National at Aintree.

The idea that an England football team making a Nazi salute might somehow help to avoid a global conflict seems more than a touch naive. Hapless administrators and players took the blame rather than ministers or diplomats. As war raged, one word stuck out. It was, indeed, futile.

There was nothing futile in trying to protect player welfare. Bert remained in football after his playing retirement to dedicate the rest of his life the care of young footballers. The former Bolton, Everton and England World Cup player, Peter Reid, joined those paying tribute to Bert Sproston. Reid began his career at Bolton Wanderers in the early 1970s just as Bert's career was ending. He described him as a 'wonderful man' who was full of 'great football stories he recited'.

Football gave Bert a living and brought him fame. Tragically, it also may have contributed to an illness that eventually claimed his life. Association football, while a contact sport, is not a collision sport in the manner of its rugby or American football counterparts. But unlike those sports, players are encouraged to use their heads to control the ball, score goals or make defensive clearances.

During the course of a career professional footballers might head the ball thousands of times in matches and training sessions. Bert Sproston retired after a long playing career interrupted by leg injuries. It never occurred to him that his brain might be at risk.

Bert's family recalled how at one moment, he would be a shining light in any room. The next, the darkness descended and sadly, he was prone to violence. Bert recognised family members, then forgot their names and deemed them to be a threat. The love of a caring family, however, endured.

His wife Renee found that she was unable to cope. Bert was hospitalised. She met up with other footballers' wives and they were joined by boxers' wives too. Bert, while fit enough to do so, helped out with the campaign. He pointed out that constantly heading an old leather football was hardly conducive to a player's long-term health. The call went out when it was too late; in some cases head injuries are still woefully treated. Bert, as an old physio, recognised the problem. It was an open and honest self-diagnosis.

His daughter-in-law, Janice, told me of his swings in mood on her visits to his hospital ward. One moment he was his old charming, warm and generous self, welcoming a beloved member of the family. The next moment, his mind went blank. As the darkness descended, he would not recognise her, and sometimes turned to violence. Family members were not safe, let alone the hospital staff caring for him. A football hero suffering symptoms likely linked to the sport he loved, the sport that gave him and others so much.

Quite whether the football family did enough for Bert and so many other footballers with Alzheimer's disease is another matter. There are countless examples. The constant heading of footballs, in Bert's day heavy leather balls soaked in water and covered in slimy mud, may well have brought on a neuro-degenerative disease. It is a struggle, even today, for some to acknowledge that the constant impact of a football on the cranium, fragile protection for the human brain, could resemble a boxing contest.

A proud, loving man brought low by those running the country and English football faced another battle. Forced to indulge Nazi propagandists, he fought back. This time a debilitating illness brought him low. Like so many souls, it was impossible to fight back. The object he loved from boyhood, the leather football, turned out probably to be a curse.

The Sproston family supported the campaigning work led by Dawn Astle, daughter of West Bromwich Albion and England centre-forward Jeff Astle. Dawn set up the Jeff Astle Foundation to raise awareness of brain injury in sport at all levels from grassroots to the elite.

Sport can promote health and fitness, certainly Bert Sproston's belief. How safeguards can be put in place, given known long-term neurological risks, is the next challenge and it will take willingness from the football authorities, both domestically and internationally. Political will is also a necessity. Politicians quite happily bask in the glory of their sports stars but that glory too often comes at a price.

As Bert Sproston lined up in Berlin's Olympiastadion to give the Nazi salute, his faith in Britain's political masters was, to put it mildly, fragile. Quite why he was ordered to do so lay in botched British diplomacy, and also deference in the age of empire to those in power.

Just what is so baffling from the years prior to war is the willingness of the FA to involve itself in the British government's rather lame use of diplomatic soft power in sport. It sustained the policy even after objections to England's footballers making the salute in Berlin. In hindsight, the England players could and should have refused point blank to give the Nazi salute but they were young men under considerable pressure from individuals in power.

For young Rolf Friedland, at least England turned up to give the land of his birth a football lesson. More importantly, his ticket to the game ended up as a ticket to freedom, given to him thanks to the intervention of one of England's Nazi-saluting players, Bert Sproston. Rolf's family will be forever grateful, an act of kindness saved his life. A UK visa in his pocket, his passenger steam train trundled out of Berlin past the observing Nazis on the station platform. It was an unlikely escape. As a refugee, Rolf successfully settled in England, becoming a fan of Sproston's old club, Tottenham Hotspur.

Ralph eventually emigrated from the UK to Israel, just one final journey.

This time, he needed no help from a random footballer. Among the projects he funded was a photography programme for special needs students. It just so happened that his saviour from Nazi tyranny featured in one of the most infamous photographs in sporting history.

Karen Pollock, chief executive of the UK's Holocaust Educational Trust, told the *Times of Israel* on 15 August 2022, 'Ralph Freeman's story is incredible. He was saved by the kindness of a stranger. Bert Sproston made a choice to stand up and be counted, and to save the life of a 17-year-old Jewish boy. Through our work with Premier League academies, we share the dark history of the Holocaust and the choices that ordinary people like Bert made across Europe. We hope these young players take stories like Ralph's and Bert's to heart and remember them for many years to come.'

Ralph's son Alan reflected on his father's values of creativity, helping others and giving back to society. Many people influenced him, nobody more so than a tough, rugged lad from Cheshire, a proud man in later life unable to remember his proud achievements, not just as a footballer but simply a human being.

Pope John Paul II, a keen sportsman, escaped the Nazis and challenged the Soviets. He once commented, 'Sport is the joy of life, a game, a celebration. It must be fostered by recovering its sheer gratuity, its ability to forge bonds of friendship, to encourage dialogue and openness towards others.'

Bert Sproston and Ralph Freeman (aka Rolf Friedland) would have agreed with such sentiments. Both saw sport, football in particular, as a source of joy, an instrument to forge friendships rather than sow division. So often, they were let down. Yet their friendship, however distant at times, served as a testament to sport for good.

Ralph Freeman told his family that he long thought back to that evening outside Berlin's Olympiastadion. He made a point of telling Bert in later life, 'If you hadn't helped me … well, I wouldn't be standing here today.' Bert responded by telling him that he did not do too much. The German-Jewish teenager did the hard part. Ralph's response? 'You gave me a chance. That's everything.'

Just one note from a happier time for English footballers than the Anglo-German international of 1938 – the World Cup of 1966. Ralph and his wife, Eva, built up a business as the UK's leading publisher of picture postcards. The FA awarded their company the franchise for World Cup Willie, the official mascot.

Bert Sproston helped Rolf Friedland/Ralph Freeman escape Nazi Germany and it inspired Ralph's charity work. Bert's kindness taught him the need to create a legacy of support for others. Unlike the Nazi monsters many in the British establishment sought to appease in the 1930s, both men epitomised the values of human decency and kindness. Then again, Bert Sproston's opponents, squealing in pain on the football field from one of his uncompromising tackles, might disagree. They still held him in awe. One of football's lesser-known stars from the wartime years, one of England's Nazi saluting players, but a talented and humane figure still to be respected.

ACKNOWLEDGEMENTS

MY GRATEFUL thanks to Alan Freeman, son of Jewish refugee Rolf Freidland/Ralph Freeman and his wife Sue Surkes. Janice Sproston, daughter-in-law of Roy Sproston for her considerable help.

And the media teams at Leeds United, Tottenham Hotspur, Manchester City and Bolton Wanderers.

SELECT BIBLIOGRAPHY

BOOKS:

Araf, Joe; *Generazione Wunderteam,* Pitch Publishing (2022)

Arendt, Hannah; *The Origins of Totalitarianism,* Penguin Ltd (1951)

Bastin, Cliff and Glanville, Brian; *Cliff Bastin Remembers,* GCR Books (2010)

Beck, Peter; *Scoring for Britain: International Football and International Politics 1900–1939,* Taylor & Francis Ltd (2013)

Buchan, Charles: *Charles Buchan, A Lifetime in Football,* Mainstream Publishing Ltd (1951, 2010)

Busby, Matt; *Soccer at the Top, My Life in Football,* Sphere Books (1974)

Butler, Bryon; *The Football League 1888–1988,* MacDonald Queen Press (1988)

Carlin, John; *Invictus: Nelson Mandela and the Game that Made a Nation,* Atlantic Books (2009)

Clay Large, David; *Nazi Games, The Olympics of 1936,* WW Norton & Co Ltd (2007)

Corbett, James; *England Expects,* Aurum Press (2006)

Cowling, Maurice; *The Impact of Hitler, British Policy and British Politics, 1933–1940,* Cambridge University Press (1975)

Clough, Matt; *Lofty, Nat Lofthouse, England's Lion of Vienna,* The History Press (2020)

Erenberg, Lewis; *The Greatest Fight of our Generation: Lewis v Schmeling*, OUP USA (2006)

Freeman, Eva; *As The Waters Flow*, Alan and Eva Freeman (2012)

Fry, Helen; *Churchill's German Army*, Lume Books (2007)

Fry, Helen; *Jews in North Devon During the Second World War*, Halsgrove (2005)

Goldblatt, David; *The Ball is Round, A Global History of Football*, Penguin Books (2007)

Green, Geoffrey; *The History of the Football Association*, Naldrett Press (1953)

Hall, David; *Manchester's Finest*, Corgi Books (2008)

Halifax, Earl of; *Fulness of Days*, Collins Ltd (1957)

Hapgood, Eddie; *Football Ambassador*, Sporting Handbooks Ltd (1945)

Hapgood, Lynne; *Eddie Hapgood Footballer: From Beyond the Touchline*, Pitch Publishing (2022)

Haywood, Paul; *England Football, The Biography*, Simon & Schuster (UK) Ltd (2022)

Hesse, Uli; *Tor! The History of German Football*, Polaris Publishing Ltd (2022)

Hyne, Ashley; *Jimmy Hogan: The Greatest Football Coach Ever?* Electric Blue Publishing (2022)

Jenkins, Roy; *Churchill*, MacMillan (2001)

Linehan, Thomas; *British Fascism 1918–39*, Manchester University Press (2000)

Leinemann, Jürgen; *Sepp Herberger. Ein Leben, eine Legende*, Rowohlt Ltd, Berlin (1997)

Matthews, Stanley; *The Way it Was*, Headline Publishing (2000)

McDonough, Frank; *The Hitler Years, Triumph 1933–1939*, Apollo (2020)

Miller, David; *Stanley Matthews, The Authorised Biography*, Pavilion Books Ltd (1989)

Nicosia, Francis R & Scrase, David; *Jewish Life in Nazi Germany*, Berghan Books (2010)

Pugh, Martin; *Hurrah for the Blackshirts*, Pimlico (2006)

Richards, Huw; *A Game For Hooligans, The History of Rugby Union;* Mainstream Publishing (2006)

Rippon, Anton; *Gas Masks for Goal Posts*, Sutton Publishing Ltd (2005)

Rose, Henry; *Before I Forget*, WH Allen Ltd (1942)

Rous, Stanley; *Football Worlds, A Lifetime in Sport*, Faber & Faber Ltd (1978)

Rollin, Jack; *Soccer at War, 1939–45*, Headline Publishing (2005)

Russell, Dave; *Football and the English*, Carnegie Publishing Ltd (1997)

Shirer, William L; *The Rise and Fall of the Third Reich, A History of Nazi Germany*, Simon & Schuster/Arrow (1960, 2011)

NEWS SOURCES

Associated Press (AP)

BBC News

BBC Sport

Belfast Telegraph, Belfast

Chester Chronicle, Chester, Cheshire

Civil and Military Gazette, Lahore

Crewe Chronicle, Crewe, Cheshire

Daily Express, London

Daily Herald, London

Daily Mail, London

Daily Mirror, London

Daily Telegraph, London

Daily Worker/Morning Star, London

Evening News, Edinburgh

Evening Sentinel, Stoke-on-Trent

Fußball Woche, Berlin, Germany

Fußball Magazin, Trossin, Germany

Hull Daily Mail, Kingston-upon-Hull

Kicker, Nuremberg, Germany

Manchester Evening Chronicle, Manchester

Manchester Evening News, Manchester

National Zeitung, Munich, Germany

Neue Freie Presse, Vienna, Austria

New York Times, New York, USA

News Chronicle, London

Press Association, London

Reuters, London

Reynolds News, London

Tageblatt, Luxembourg

The Scotsman, Edinburgh

Times of Israel, Jerusalem

Völkischer Beobachter, Munich, Germany

Western Daily Press, Bristol

Yorkshire Post, Leeds

ARCHIVE and OFFICIAL SOURCES

British Library, London, explore.bl.uk/

Football Association, Wembley, London, www.thefa.com/

Football and War Network, www.wlv.ac.uk/research/research-centres/centre-for-historical-research/football-and-war-network/

Hansard (UK Parliament), Westminster, hansardparliament.uk/Commons

International Olympic Committee, Lausanne, www.olympic.org/theioc

National Football Museum, Manchester, https://www.nationalfootballmuseum.com/

UK National Archives, Kew, London, nationalarchives.gov.uk/

CAB 23-93, CAB 24-240, FO 954-10A, FO 395-568, FO 371-, HO 45-16425